Front cover: Ex-LMS Stanier Black 5 4-6-0 no. 45407 The Lancashire Fusilier *and BR Riddles Standard class 4 2-6-0 'Mogul' no. 76079 double head the return Carlisle - Hellifield Goods Loop section of the 'Christmas Dalesman' railtour en route to Bedford on 29th December 2005. The Black 5 was named at Bolton Street station, Bury, and resides on the East Lancashire Railway. The Mogul is now stored on the North Yorkshire Moors Railway awaiting an overhaul. (Dick Manton)*

Back cover pictures:
Upper: At an altitude of 1,150ft (350m) Dent station is the highest operational railway station on the national network in England. The shot of the board on the up platform, taken on 30th May 1983, marks this record. Note the snow fence behind the board. (Tom Heavyside)

Lower: BR Brush Type 4 Co-Co class 47 no. 47479 at Dent station is hauling a Leeds - Carlisle stopping service on 9th June 1984. (Tom Heavyside)

Back cover map: Railway Clearing House map, dated 1947, edited. The route of the album is shown with a dotted line.

Title page: This plaque is located on the up platform on Settle station as seen on 21st October 2021. (Michael Ellis)

ACKNOWLEDGEMENTS

I am very grateful for the assistance received from those mentioned in the credits, also from Paul Crook, Godfrey Croughton, Cumbria Railways Association, Rob Daniels, Gordon Edgar, Geoff Gartside, Bryan Gray, Chris Howard, Don Jary, Norman Langridge, Cass Morgan, Jane Moriarty, Pete Myers, Brian Read, David and Dr Susan Salter, Paul Shannon, Michael Stewart, and Dave Stubbins.

Published December 2024

ISBN 978 1 910356 89 0

© Middleton Press Ltd, 2024

Cover design and Photographic enhancement
  Deborah Esher
Production Cassandra Morgan

Published by
  Middleton Press Ltd
  Camelsdale Road
  Haslemere
  Surrey
  GU27 3RJ
Tel: 01730 813169
Email: info@middletonpress.co.uk
www.middletonpress.co.uk

Printed by 4Bind Ltd, Unit B Caxton Point,
Caxton Way, Stevenage, Hertfordshire SG1 2XU
Telephone +44 (0) 1438 745005; www.4bind.co.uk

Abbreviations:
BR - British Rail
DfT - Department for Transport
FoSCL - Friends of the Settle - Carlisle Line
IBS - Intermediate Block Signal
L&CR - Lancaster and Carlisle Railway
LNWR - London and North Western Railway
LSL - Locomotive Services Ltd
MG&SW - Midland, Glasgow &
           South Western Railway
MP - Milepost
Midland - Midland Railway
NER - North Eastern Railway
NR - Network Rail
NWR - North Western Railway
WCML - West Coast Main Line
WCR West Coast Railway
WWI - World War I
WWII - World War II

SECTIONS

CONTENTS

I. The Railway Clearing House map (edited) of 1947 has the route of this album in red.

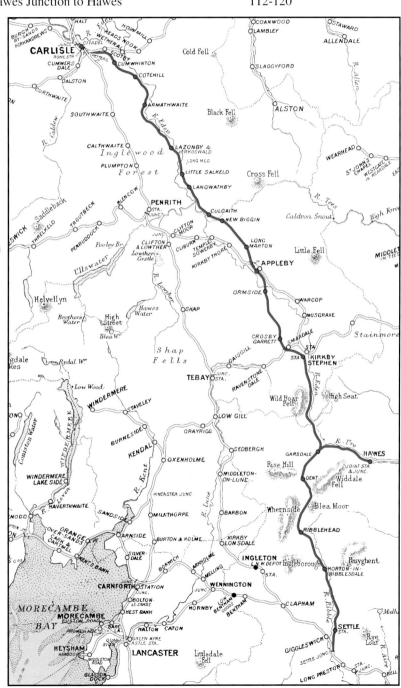

GEOGRAPHICAL SETTING

O.S. Nock wrote: 'This line is the only mountain railway in the world that was built for express trains', which is evidenced by the way in which the Settle & Carlisle line was prodigiously engineered to pass through the stunning and often very bleak features of the Yorkshire Dales and North Pennines. These include some of England's highest peaks and deep valleys that, in the end, required no less than 14 tunnels and 22 viaducts to be constructed, including the iconic Ribblehead viaduct. It is a line that boasts the highest operational station in England, Dent, and at one time reputedly had the highest water troughs in the world at Garsdale. The aforementioned engineering was such that it allowed express trains to run on the line by ensuring no gradient was greater than 1 in 100 or curves too sharp to restrict speed. The Ribble and Eden rivers provided a natural route through the hills for a railway line but the terrain and climate created huge obstacles during construction. Likened to a beached whale, the line climbs the 16 mile (26km) section rapidly from Settle Junction to Blea Moor most of which is at the ruling gradient of 1 in 100. This was referred to as 'the Long Drag' by footplate men. Thereafter, the line undulates until it reaches its summit at Ais Gill just north of Garsdale at 1,169ft (356m) above sea level. After that, the line drops gradually down the 56 miles (90km) of the Eden Valley before reaching Carlisle. North of Settle, the line passes Pen-y-Ghent 2,277ft (694m) to the east; Ingleborough 2,372ft (723m) to the west and, after crossing the Ribblehead Viaduct, Whernside 2,415ft (736m), the last of the 'three Peaks', again to the west. As the line continues north, Wild Boar Fell 2,323ft (708m) overlooking the Mallerstang Valley, Murton Pike 1,949ft (594m) the Eden Valley and finally Cross Fell, the highest mountain in the Pennines at 2,930ft (893m), are all passed providing stunning backdrops to the line.

From Settle the line passes through carboniferous limestone almost as far as Appleby encountering outcrops of millstone grit on the way, reflecting the quarrying operations along the route. Thereafter, it is a mix of Penrith sands and Eden shale that contains deposits of gypsum that was mined at Kirkby Thore, Long Meg and Cotehill. Both the mining of gypsum and manufacture of gypsum products continue at Kirkby Thore. Other industries along the line include livestock farming; many stations had cattle docks. Today, tourism is booming, and has become one of the main industries.

Because much of the line's route was dictated by the terrain, it means that a number of stations are somewhat remote from the villages whose names they bear. In 1991, the entire line was granted conservation area status, which was the result of combined action by the Yorkshire Dales National Park Authority, Craven District, Eden District and Carlisle City Councils. With a total length of 78 miles (126km) between Hellifield and Carlisle and a width of never more than a few hundred yards, it claims to be the longest such area in Britain. The Settle & Carlisle Line is testament to the Midland Railway Company's (Midland's) ambitious feats of engineering and construction that has left its mark on the countryside and provides a perfect contrast between natural beauty and bold man-made structures.

Unless otherwise stated all maps and diagrams used are Midland 'two chains to the inch' Land Plans reproduced by courtesy of the Midland Railway Study Centre, Derby. All plans are dated between 1911-12.

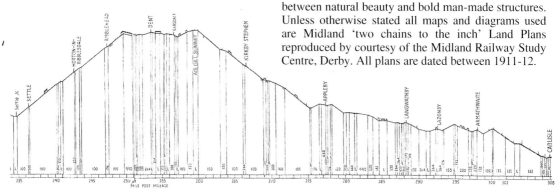

HISTORICAL BACKGROUND

In 1840, Lord Melbourne's government set up the Smith-Barlow Commission in response to extensive public and commercial interest to make recommendations for the most effective railway route to Scotland. Despite this, the commission's conclusion, published on 15th March 1841, assumed that only one line linking England and Scotland would be required. While the committee was deliberating, work was already ongoing on what was to become the West Coast Main Line (WCML) reaching Glasgow in 1848 and, similarly, during the 1830s and 1840s the East Coast Main line was also under construction. The committee had no mandatory powers and the rest, as they say, is history. By then the Midland was expanding: south to London and north to gain a foothold in Yorkshire, which was seen as a valuable stepping stone to Scotland.

Despite the typical railway politics and rivalry of the day, the Midland's plan to reach Scotland turned on an association with the London and North Western Railway (LNWR). To reach that point, the Midland first acquired the Leeds and Bradford Extension Railway that ran as far west as Skipton and later the 'Little' North Western Railway (NWR), which had plans to build a line from Skipton to Low Gill on the Lancaster and Carlisle Railway (L&CR) by then under control of the LNWR.

The line between Skipton and Ingleton opened on 31st July 1849; however, due to lack of funds construction of the Ingleton - Low Gill section was suspended and, thereafter, the NWR concentrated on developing the line from Clapham Junction towards Morecambe via Lancaster. For the time being, the Midland's hopes of reaching Scotland were dashed; so much so that the short Clapham - Ingleton stub was closed less than a year after it opened.

But all was not lost. After much to-ing and fro-ing between the companies concerned, in June 1857 a Commons Committee accepted proposals from the L&CR to undertake construction of the suspended, effectively abandoned, Ingleton - Low Gill line. It opened to passengers on 16th September 1861 but nothing was straightforward. Unable to reach agreement for shared use of the Midland station at Ingleton, the LNWR opened its own just beyond the northern end of the substantial 800yds (732 m), 11 arch viaduct over the River Greta. This required through passengers to walk between the two stations and negotiate the slopes of the river valley in order to gain a connection. By 1862 the LNWR trains at last ran through to the Midland station but services were slow and the LNWR was accused of deliberately mistiming its trains, resulting in poor connections with Midland services. As a consequence, the promised through trains to Scotland never materialised despite the line being capable of accommodating express traffic.

The ongoing dispute between the Midland and the LNWR led to a decision by the Midland Board to establish a third route to Scotland. After an initial survey in 1865 an Act of Parliament, strongly opposed by the LNWR, was passed in June 1866 permitting construction of what was to become the Settle & Carlisle line but once again nothing was straightforward. The UK was in a state of financial torpor and the railway industry was faring no better, including the Midland, to the extent that its Board wanted to abandon the venture. This was for good reason as the LNWR finally proposed a workable deal to allow the Midland running powers over its route to the north; a deal conditional upon the latter applying for an Abandonment Bill. In the face of much opposition from the Midland's railway associates and shareholders, the application for abandonment was turned down and Parliament insisted the Act of 1866 be implemented. In effect, the Directors of the Midland were pushed into the project almost certainly against their better judgement.

At last the Settle & Carlisle line was to become a reality, although strictly speaking it only runs as far north to Petteril Bridge Junction at Durranhill where it meets the North Eastern Railway (NER) Tyne Valley line. Construction of the line began in 1869 and was planned to take four years but it dragged on for a further 2½ years much to the frustration of the Midland Board. The line was eventually opened for freight traffic in August 1875, which helped bed it down prior to the commencement of passenger services on 1st May 1876. It was an incredible achievement given the appalling weather conditions recorded during construction, including frequent storms, high winds, snow lying in shaded areas as late as June and average annual rainfall of 70ins (178cm); the remoteness of much of the line and the unforgiving terrain were further aggravating factors.

There are many names associated with this engineering and construction marvel but there were two notables, namely: James Allport, General Manager of the Midland, who presided over the problematic venture to ensure that the Company could secure a direct share of the remunerative Scottish traffic, and John Crossley, Chief Engineer of the Midland, who postponed his retirement so he could oversee construction of the line as engineer-in-chief; he was hailed a hero by W.R. Mitchell in his book, *How they Built the Settle-Carlisle Railway*. A third was Tasmanian, Charles Sharland, recruited by John Crossley from the Maryport & Carlisle Railway. In 10 days, despite being snowed up for several of them, Charles Sharland walked the whole of the proposed route making preliminary surveys along the way. Clearly he was one of the line's pioneers but not long after his achievement he developed tuberculosis and died at the young age of 26; sadly he never saw the finished result of his efforts.

Parliament's decision to reject the Abandonment Bill led to the rapid re-instatement of the Midland's construction committee, now it was obliged to build the line, and soon after it started drafting and issuing contracts for the work. There were five in all: Contract No. 1: Settle Junction to Dent Head awarded in September 1869; Contract No. 2: Dent Head to Kirkby Stephen - November 1869; Contract No. 3: Smardale to Crowdundle - March 1870; Contract No. 4: Crowdundle to Durranhill - April 1870 and Contract No. 5: for the 6 mile (9.7km) Hawes Branch in mid-1871. This meant all sections of the line were being built more or less simultaneously and it avoided the Midland putting all its eggs in one basket contractor-wise. For consistency, the sections following in this album are based on the sections covered by these contracts.

The Settle & Carlisle line was the last main line railway to be constructed in Britain for some considerable time; an immense effort using primarily manual labour in numbers that rose to over 6,000 at peak. The workers were accommodated in large camps at various points along the route, some with exotic sounding names such as Jericho and Sebastapol; the largest was Batty Green near Ribblehead that accommodated over 2,000 men. Some of the camps were large enough to include schools, post offices and places of worship. Sadly over 100 perished during construction and others due to such things as smallpox; for instance 80 died of the disease at Batty Green. There are memorials along the line to commemorate lost workmen notably at St. Leonard's church in Chapel-le-Dale and St. Mary's at Mallerstang.

There are numerous instances of major obstacles encountered during construction and these are covered throughout in further notes and picture captions. Many resulted in cuttings becoming tunnels and embankments viaducts in order to maintain the standard features that gradients should not exceed 1 in 100 and the sharp curves avoided; the consequences of which required major engineering changes that increased significantly the cost of construction. The original budget for the line was £2.2 million set by the Midland but the final figure amounted to £3.5m (or about £500m in today's money), which seems very low compared with estimates for (say) HS2. This is probably accounted for by the fact that the line was effectively built by hand and light on mechanical equipment, technology and other factors that prevail today.

Including the short-lived Settle Junction station, the Midland built 20 stations; the most northerly being Scotby. All station buildings were fairly modest affairs constructed in what was referred to as Midland or Derby gothic design, notable mainly for the steeply pitched roofs (the gothic feature). Railway workers' cottages and station buildings were the creation of the Midland's architect, John Holloway Sanders. The single-storey station buildings were designed in three variants: large - reserved for the market towns en route such as Settle; medium - as seen at Armathwaite and small - Ribblehead and were built in the local stone quarried along the route. In an article for the Settle Carlisle Railway Conservation Area, Mark R. Harvey writes, 'an easy way to distinguish between the three variants: count the number of chimney stacks - 4 for large, 3 for medium and 2 for small'. In most cases the only building of note on the opposite platforms would have been a simple shelter in similar if limited design. The stations were rather modest affairs compared with the grand edifices and natural features of the line. All stations would have had a station master's house, some railway workers' cottages nearby and in many cases a goods yard and signal box, with other boxes located at strategic points, notably at Blea Moor and Ais Gill. Today only 10 of the original stations remain open for business.

Had bitter rivalry not carried the day between the Midland and LNWR the line may never have come to be or should perhaps not have been built on financial grounds, but completed it was, and the Midland, under the stewardship of James Allport, was not going to rest on its laurels. New generations of locomotives were procured in particular to negotiate the Long Drag such as those designed by Johnson, Kirtley and, later, Deeley, although some would argue they were underpowered for the task in hand. The Midland's reputation for comfort was also enhanced with such things as the introduction of Pullman coaches, not a total success, and the abolition of 3rd class throughout, except perhaps on some through coaches from a variety of locations such as Bristol. The line prospered from day one perhaps peaking around the WWI years and after, but from the 1923 Grouping, that saw the creation of the London Midland and Scottish Railway (LMS), it was clear that the Settle & Carlisle route to Scotland was unable to compete successfully with the WCML due to its steeper gradients, longer distance and the number of stops involved serving major cities such as: Leicester, Derby, Nottingham, Sheffield and Leeds. Nationalisation of the railways in 1948 saw the pace of a rundown quicken, although the line was used extensively to test various forms of motive power. By the 1960s the writing was on the wall with closure of the route looming, and the through services to London were run down, ending in the 1970s.

While some stations closed in the 1940s and 1950s, in May 1970 British Rail (BR) closed all remaining stations apart from Settle and Appleby with passenger services cut to two trains a day in each direction. Freight traffic continued but by 1983 a good deal had been diverted on to the WCML as much of the line's infrastructure was deteriorating. With revenues dropping drastically for obvious reasons, BR came to the conclusion that the all-in cost of £12m for repairing and, in some cases, renewing viaducts and tunnels would not be a viable proposition. The centrepiece of BR's closure case was the spectacular viaduct at Ribblehead, which was said to be in danger of collapse and too expensive to repair at an estimate of £6m; so, in 1984 BR posted Settle & Carlisle line closure notices. This was clearly a case of closure by stealth first intimated some 18 years earlier, when the line's demise was mentioned in an official report concerning an accident involving two freight trains near Horton-in-Ribblesdale.

In response to the demands of fell walkers, ramblers and enthusiasts alike, following the closure of stations in 1970, the DalesRail service began in 1974. The service operated in daylight hours stopping at the previously closed stations - a precursor perhaps to the line's later revival.

When the likelihood of closure of the line became apparent, Graham Nuttall and David Burton created the Friends of the Settle - Carlisle Line (FoSCL) that held its inaugural meeting in Settle Town Hall in June 1981 long before any formal announcement was made by BR. There were a great many people involved in saving the Settle & Carlisle line; too many to mention for fear of missing someone but there was one person in particular, Ron Cotton, creator of the Saver fare, BR Project Manager for the line, who could perhaps be described as gamekeeper turned poacher. His responsibility was simply to oversee the withdrawal of train services and closure of the line. However given that the procedure to implement the statutory requirements for closure is a long and drawn out process, the opportunity arose to market and promote the line, which he did making use of his entrepreneurial skills. His efforts primarily, supported by many groups and individuals and a public enquiry, were the major influences in the government's 1989 decision to withdraw the proposal to close the line; there had been over 20,000 written objections to the closure. The public outcry and successful efforts to market the line resulted in the Secretary of State for Transport announcing on 11th April 1989 that consent for closure of the Settle & Carlisle, along with the associated Hellifield - Blackburn line, would be refused. The announcement saw BR start to carry out much needed repairs and maintenance on various tunnels and viaducts as well as the re-opening of stations. By the time Ron retired seven years later his contribution spoke for itself; passenger services had increased from two to five trains a day in each direction and eight stations, closed in 1970, were reopened and later brought up to standard to accommodate the new timetable. Passenger numbers had increased five-fold and the revelation that, with the trial repair of one arch on the Ribblehead Viaduct, the cost of full repair would be much lower than originally estimated by BR. In 2020 the then chair of FoSCL, Paul Brown, wrote in its Journal about the recent passing of Ron Cotton: 'The best fitting tribute I can make for this Officer and Gentleman is taken from the wording on the tomb of Christopher Wren in St Paul's Cathedral, London - "If you seek his memorial, look all around you".'

Freight has always been and still is a significant factor in the line's history to the extent that, in 2025, it celebrates the 150th anniversary of its opening for freight traffic, preceding passenger traffic by almost a year. Freight traffic declined over the years but was resurrected in the early 1990s with the desulphogypsum trains to Kirkby Thore from Drax power station. Soon afterwards coal traffic started running from Hunterston's deep water terminal and Scottish opencast mines to power stations in the Aire and Trent valleys. At its height, coal traffic amounted to several trains a day that warranted the line being open on a three-shift basis. However, the traffic declined gradually as coal-fired power stations were decommissioned with the last of the regular coal trains running in 2015. The line is also host to a variety of other freight services, such as: the log trains rostered at Carlisle bound for Chirk; delivery of imported gypsum to Kirkby Thore, replacing the former service from Drax and cement trains heading north from the Ribblesdale plant in Clitheroe. Stone trains have continued from Arcow, Ribblehead and, from 2025, will start running from Horton quarry.

At one time the line between Settle and Petteril Bridge Junctions boasted over 30 manual signal boxes. Today only seven remain, plus the later panel cabin at Kirkby Thore, and the line is still home to a mixture of semaphore and colour light signals. Piecemeal closure of signal boxes from the 1960s to the 1980s created long headways, which suited the dwindling traffic at the time, but later hindered an upturn in the Anglo - Scottish coal traffic. From 2007-10 axle counters and intermediate block signals were added on both the Settle & Carlisle line and Annan-Mauchline section of the former Glasgow & South Western line to counter this. Those changes provided all the capacity the line is likely to need for the foreseeable future. In 2011, Network Rail (NR) forecast closure of all the line's operational boxes by 2020 with a view to centralising control of the North West from a new Rail Operating Centre in Ashburys, Manchester, but all still remain. Since then priorities have changed, focusing on the need to replace a number of power boxes installed in the 1970s and 1980s. Ironically, as a result of this action, the Settle and Carlisle line boxes have outlived an era of signalling that has all but been eradicated elsewhere.

Like all main lines the Settle & Carlisle was not immune from accidents and mishaps some of which resulted in a number of fatalities. Some of the earlier accidents were considered due to the Midland policy of using relatively small locomotives that had barely sufficient power to deal with the steep gradients on the line without assistance of banking engines. Mention of the various accidents is made throughout this album. In February 2016 torrential rain caused a 500,000 tonnes landslip near Armathwaite that completely blocked the line. NR embarked on an immense £23m project to reinstate the line, which did not re-open until March 2017. To mark the occasion 12 services were operated by Northern with trains between Appleby and Skipton hauled by A1 Pacific no. 60163 *Tornado*. More recently in October 2022 five cement powder wagons on a Clitheroe - Carlisle service became derailed at Petteril Bridge of which two fell into the river. As a consequence, the lines to both Leeds and Newcastle were blocked for seven weeks due to the difficult recovery operation and damage to the track and bridge.

At present NR owns and maintains the operational infrastructure of the line, including track, signalling, buildings and structures for the use by passenger services and freight operators and Northern is the current Train Operating Company. In addition there are four groups that support the line in a variety of ways both separately and 'in partnership'.

Since its formation in 1981, the FoSCL has developed into an organisation that provides train guides and station volunteers, funding of station improvements, runs the station shops at Appleby and Settle, operates and maintains station buildings at Dent as holiday lets and supports the funding of projects by other organisations.

The Settle & Carlisle Railway Trust is a registered charity formed in 1990 that focuses on the line's activity between Hellifield and Carlisle to preserve, restore and maintain historic buildings and structures along the route. It promotes public knowledge and appreciation of the line and access to historic buildings. The trust has long-term property leases from NR and also operates holiday lets at a number of stations along the route, such as those at: Horton-in-Ribblesdale, Ribblehead and Kirkby Stephen and has promoted seasonal cafés at Horton and Ribblehead.

The Settle-Carlisle Railway Development Company Limited incorporated in 1992 is responsible for marketing and supporting the scheduled services on the line and encouraging appropriate sustainable development along the line's corridor. It operates the refreshment trolleys on passenger services and deals also with group bookings on behalf of Northern and supplements the opening hours of the ticket offices at both Appleby and Settle stations. Most significantly it is the official Community Rail Partner for the line supported by both the Department for Transport (DfT) and Northern.

The Settle Carlisle Railway Conservation Area stakeholders aim to preserve and enhance the line's character and appearance, by making sustainable decisions about its future and countering threats of incremental and dramatic change due to neglect caused by economic decline, as well as over-investment and pressure for development.

Regional Railways was created in 1982 and was one of the three passenger sectors of BR that existed until 1997 two years after the privatisation of the UK's railways. It was succeeded by First North Western that operated the North West Regional Railways franchise from March 1997 until December 2004. Northern Rail branded as 'Northern', was a train operating company owned by Serco-Abellio that operated the franchise from 2004 until 2016. Arriva Rail North, again branded as Northern, began operating the franchise on 1st April 2016 but it was terminated early by the DfT in January 2020 amid widespread dissatisfaction over its performance, particularly in respect of poorly implemented timetable changes. As a consequence, the franchise was taken into government ownership. The Northern area of operation is huge and diverse to the extent that the line has not always enjoyed top priority but, on the plus side, privatisation has given rise to the line's Community Rail Partnership.

Today the line is as popular as ever with tourists, walkers and rail enthusiasts; many books have been published and songs written reflecting its continued attraction. All remaining stations along the line have been refurbished to a high standard reflecting the line's Midland legacy; in fact, the stations would not look out of place on any heritage line across the country. On the downside perhaps but for good reason, the line is subject to a speed restriction of 60mph (96kph) throughout. The line is also host to a variety of steam and diesel excursions, which rarely if ever stop at any intermediate stations other than occasionally Appleby to take on water; while they do not generate income for the businesses on the line, their presence perhaps acts as a catalyst for others to visit. Freight and passenger services are rarely diverted on to the line these days because the drivers of other train operating companies do not have the appropriate route knowledge.

The Settle & Carlisle line still plays an important role in the national network perhaps best evidenced by the £23m spent repairing the Armathwaite landslip. It has its anomalies such as southbound quarry services having to travel north in order reverse at Blea Moor. Most of all, the enthusiasm and persistence that saved the line back in the 1980s persists to this day in the form of the various organisations set up to secure its existence hopefully way into the future. O.S. Nock, described the line as 'Britain's Most Spectacular Main Line' and few surely would argue with that.

PASSENGER SERVICES

In April 2026, the Settle & Carlisle Line will celebrate the 150th anniversary of the first passenger services but, even back then, the route was considered a main line with local traffic more or less relegated to secondary status due in part to the fact that a number stations were some distance from the villages they purported to serve. In 1927 the LMS introduced the London - Glasgow 'Thames - Clyde' express that ran fast from Leeds to Carlisle and in the same year the London - Edinburgh 'Thames - Forth' express service was introduced; in 1957 it was renamed the 'Waverley', stopping at Settle and Appleby en route to Carlisle. The Waverley ceased to run during the winter after 1964 but continued to operate during the summer months until September 1968. With cessation of the Waverley service, the Thames - Clyde added coaches for Edinburgh and made additional stops at Settle and Appleby; it continued until 1976. After that, through services from Glasgow continued, but only as far as Nottingham, surviving until May 1982. In the early 1970s all services were cut back drastically as BR was looking to close the line with only Settle and Appleby stations remaining open. The grand turnaround in favour of passengers began in 1974 when DalesRail services were introduced stopping at some of the closed stations. However, in order to restore full passenger services, eight stations had to be refurbished and, in the case of Ribblehead, the down platform had to be re-instated. In the summer months of 2020, Rail Charter Services operated the first-class only luxury service: 'The North Pennines Staycation Express' between Skipton and Appleby and again in 2021 when it ran through to Carlisle. Due to circumstances beyond the operator's control the 2022 service was suspended. From the outset of passenger services, there were five Leeds - Carlisle trains in each direction; whereas today there are six benefitting from a substantial influx of tourists, walkers and enthusiasts. In June 2024, in addition to the regular Leeds - Carlisle traffic, Northern introduced a summer Saturday-only service between Rochdale and Ribblehead known as the 'Yorkshire Dales Explorer'; the return service runs twice on a Saturday via Manchester Victoria, Clitheroe and Hellifield to Settle, Horton-in-Ribblesdale and Ribblehead.

1. Settle Junction to Dent Head Viaduct
17 miles and 18 chains (27.7km)

The contract for construction of this section of the line was awarded to John Ashwell of London in September 1869 for approximately £350,000. Unfortunately he ran into financial difficulties and in October 1871 his contract was taken over by the Midland Railway. Up to 2,300 men were employed on this section during construction.

Settle Junction

Situated some 39¾ miles (64km) northwest of Leeds the Settle & Carlisle line diverges to the north towards Settle between Long Preston and Giggleswick stations on the former 'Little' North Western Railway. The junction completed in 1874 marks the start of the climb to Blea Moor and Ais Gill known as the 'Long Drag'. Today the junction is marked by the Midland Type 4c signal box that can be seen from the A65, which runs alongside the line at this point. Originally there were two boxes: Settle Junction South opened in 1894, itself replacing a box from 1874, that closed in 1923 and the current box that opened in 1913. The box was reframed in 1960 and controls the busy double junction that was reconfigured as a ladder arrangement due to a derailment in 1979. Incidentally, the line between Settle Junction and Carnforth is the longest block section on the UK rail network at just over 24 miles (39km).

1. Preserved ex-LMS Stanier Jubilee class 4-6-0 no. 5593 (BR 45593) *Kolhapur* heads the Cumbrian Mountain Express through Settle Junction at the start of the Long Drag in February 1987. In June 2024 it was announced that *Kolhapur* was sold to the West Coast Railway Company (WCR) to be part of its mainline steam fleet. (Dick Manton)

SETTLE JUNCTION STATION

II. Opened in November 1876 between Long Preston and Giggleswick on the former 'Little' NWR as an exchange station with the route to Morecambe. It was not a commercial success and the station closed on 1st November 1877.

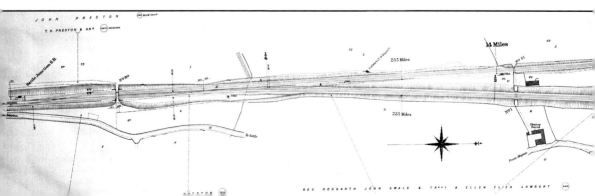

SETTLE

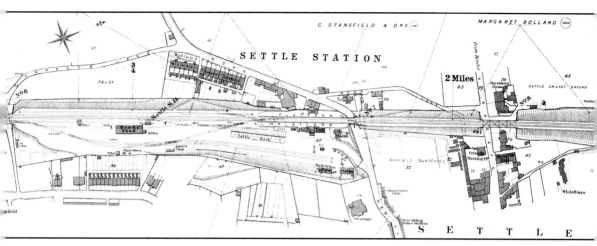

III. This plan shows the station layout c1912. Compared with today the station is in a fairly rural setting. It opened on 1st May 1876 as Settle New and on 1st July 1879 was renamed Settle. The station is situated in the heart of the market town, which has another station, Giggleswick, formerly Settle Old, situated on the Leeds - Morecambe line. The station is typical of the larger building designed by the Midland's architect John Sanders and was Grade II listed on 9th March 1984. Reaching the northbound platform was originally by way of the barrow crossing to the north of the station but following electrification of the East Coast mainline, the footbridge at Prestonpans was dismantled and re-erected at Settle. The barrow crossing is still accessible by wheelchair users etc when the station is staffed. Goods facilities were withdrawn 12th October 1970 and the water tower in the former yard was converted into residential accommodation in 2011. The first signal box was opened on 2nd August 1875, replaced in 1891 closed in 1984 and was moved in June 1997 to its present site by the Friends of the Settle & Carlisle Line and is open to the public on most Saturdays. In January 1960, just north of Settle station at milepost 237 near the village of Langcliffe, the locomotive hauling a southbound express shed its connecting rod that damaged the opposite track to the extent it derailed an oncoming goods train. There were five fatalities and eight injured.

← 2. In this shot c1925 a Midland Railway Belpaire super-heated class 700 4-4-0 no. 736 is seen heading an up express through Settle. The second vehicle is an ex-LNWR 6-wheel passenger brake van and the following carriage may be an ex-LNWR vehicle too. When the new LMS standard carriages entered service on the WCML older LNWR corridor vehicles started being cascaded to other parts of the Midland. (Robert Humm coll.)

➜ *World War I farewell scene at Settle station on 2nd September 1914. (John Alsop collection)*

3. Shortly after the installation of the aforementioned footbridge reconditioned at Newton Heath BR class 156 DMU Super Sprinter no.156475 is seen entering the station on 10th April 1993 with a late afternoon Carlisle to Leeds service. The footbridge was relocated from Prestonpans station in East Lothian. (Noel Machell)

4. A rare photograph of the 'Minimodal' concept at Settle station on 28th August 2002. The Megafret twin intermodal wagons sandwiched between BR BRCW Type 3 Bo-Bo Cromptons nos 33030 and 33025 in Direct Rail Services livery is loaded with 12 'Minimodal' cube containers that can be handled by overhead crane or a fork-lift truck. Each container had two solid sides and two roller shutter doors and could be loaded any way on the wagon, providing security for high-value goods. As can be seen in this image, the concept matched the 'Megafret' wagon perfectly aligned with the platform height, making it ideal for mail and parcels traffic. Unfortunately, Royal Mail withdrew from rail shortly after this and another innovative solution for railfreight was lost. Minimodal innovator Theodore Bird is standing on the platform during a filming session prior to the concept launch at the National Railway Museum being one of the Strategic Rail Authority 'Railfreight Innovation Award' winners of 2000. (Gordon Edgar)

5. After leaving Settle station the line passes over the Whitefriars viaduct and then Marshfield viaduct seen in this shot. In an attempt to make up for lost time, ex-LMS Stanier Royal Scot class 4-6-0 no. 46115 *Scots Guardsman* hurries past the Marshfield Ground of the Settle cricket club ground in charge of the Carnforth - Carlisle 'The Lune Rivers Trust Special' during an unexpected brief spell of sunshine on 4th October 2014. The cricket club was founded in 1842. (Gordon Edgar)

Stainforth Tunnel

Shortly after leaving Settle the line passes through Stainforth also known as Taitlands tunnel - the southernmost tunnel on the line and the fourth shortest at just 120 yards (110m).

Sheriff Brow viaducts

6. At this point there are two viaducts: Little Sheriff Brow at 55yds (50m) long, 25ft (7.6m) high with three arches and, just to the south, Sheriff Brow at 58yds (53m) long, 55ft (16.8m) high, again with three arches. The 'Cathedrals Express', seen here on 25th August 2011, is hauled by BR Riddles Standard 'Britannia' class 7 4-6-2 no. 70013 *Oliver Cromwell*. It is crossing the River Ribble by way of the Little Sheriff Brow viaduct. (Dick Manton)

Craven Lime Company's Quarry & Lime Kilns and Stainforth Sidings

A few miles north of Settle just past Langcliffe Paper Mill, now a retail outlet, the line passes the former Craven Lime Co's quarry and works and Stainforth sidings. The site is now a visitor attraction highlighting in particular the various types of kilns that heated the limestone in order to make mortar.

The Stainforth sidings were controlled by the signal box, which opened on 2nd August 1875, was later replaced in 1898 and again in 1950. It was taken out of use on 29th September 1963, soon demolished, and was replaced by an Intermediate Block Signal (IBS). The Craven Lime Company's Sidings also boasted a signal box; this opened in June 1877 and closed in July 1901 and was later demolished.

7. BR Brush Traction Type 4 Class 47 Co-Co no. D1737 (TOPS no. 47144), in two-tone green, hauls 7M31, a mixed freight train from (Leeds) Hunslet to Carlisle. It is seen alongside the river Ribble as it passes the siding for the Helwith Bridge Granite Company on 29th March 1968. The siding was controlled by a ground frame, which was installed in 1926 and taken out of use on 7th September 1969. (Noel Machell)

Helwith Bridge Signal Box

Located more or less opposite the site of the Arcow sidings; it opened on 11th April 1876, was replaced on 21st August 1896 and closed on 7th September 1969 and later demolished.

Helwith Bridge

8. Ex-LMS Stanier Princess Royal class 4-6-2 no. 6201 (BR 46201) *Princess Elizabeth*, in LMS red livery, together with no. 97251 ETHEL2 (formerly BR Sulzer class 25 no. 25305) double-head the northbound 'Pennine Pullman' service on 7th February 1987. (Tom Heavyside)

Dry Rigg and Arcow Quarries

These two quarries are adjacent to each other to the west of the line opposite Helwith Bridge; the Arcow quarry is the northerly of the two. Siltstone is extracted from both facilities and is used primarily for high speed roads and airport runways; there are only six sources of this type of rock in the UK and so the operator, a Lafarge-Tarmac joint venture, is keen to extend quarrying operations but to do so the Yorkshire Dales National Park Authority required the operator to minimise road haulage and maximise the use of rail to transport quarry products, including establishing rail links at the three quarries in Ribblesdale. The third quarry is at Horton-in-Ribblesdale, covered later in this album.

9. Work commenced on the siding serving the Dry Rigg and the Arcow quarries in July 2015 and on 26th January 2016 GB Railfreight hauled the first trainload of roadstone out of Arcow quarry after a 50 year hiatus. Class 66 no. 66757, after arriving with the 22.04 Bredbury - Arcow turn, will later form the 12.12 Arcow - Pendleton service on 19th October 2016. Shunting is in progress because the wagon rake needs to be split between the three sidings. The wagons are former coal hoppers repurposed for stone. The terminal sends out roughly five trains a week and the regular destinations are Pendleton, Bredbury and Leeds Hunslet. (Paul Shannon)

10. In the background, GB Railfreight in Biffa red branding class 66 no. 66783 *The Flying Dustman* heads past Arcow with the 6M38 11.25 Arcow Quarry to Bredbury having reversed at Blea Moor. Meanwhile, classmate no. 66782 reverses into the loading sidings with its empty hopper wagons having arrived on 6M31 09.53 Hunslet Tilcon to Arcow Quarry on 23rd August 2022. So much heavy freight traffic kept off the roads with just these two trains alone. These two consecutively numbered class 66s in the GB Railfreight fleet were purchased from DB Cargo in early 2018, 66046 and 66058 becoming 66782 and 66783, respectively. (Gordon Edgar)

Horton Quarry

Horton Quarry is a source of limestone to the southwest of Horton-in-Ribblesdale station; it has been operating since at least 1889 and produces limestone for a variety of purposes. The quarry lost its rail connection in February 1965 and in recent years stone has been transported by lorry to the sidings at Ribblehead station for onward carriage by rail. In line with agreements reached with the Yorkshire Dales National Park Authority, 2025 will see the reinstatement of the rail connection to Horton Quarry via a branch off the main line at Horton-in-Ribblesdale station.

Seen on a visit to the quarry on 11th June 1962 revealed an out of use Hudswell Clarke 0-6-0 saddle tank bearing the name Margeret *and a works plate no. 1468 built in 1921. There is no record of this locomotive surviving in preservation. (Noel Machell)*

HORTON-IN-RIBBLESDALE

IV. Opened as Horton on 1st May 1876 this station was renamed Horton-in-Ribblesdale by the LMS on 26th September 1927. This was one of the stations closed by BR in 1970 but as a result of the concerted efforts of campaigners the station re-opened on 16th July 1986. In the 1950s and 1960s under stationmaster, Mr James Taylor, won the 'Best Kept Station' award for 17 consecutive years. The station was restored by the Settle & Carlisle Railway Trust and the gardens tended by volunteers. In 2022 Network Rail embarked on a scheme to replace the current foot crossing at the station with a modern footbridge complete with lifts that will be fully commissioned in early 2025. The crossing has an average of 3,000 users a day including those taking part in the Three Peaks Challenge where the footpath linking two of the peaks, Ingleborough with Pen-y-ghent, traverses the line. The station signal box was opened on 2nd August 1875; it was replaced in August 1896; closed in 1984 and burned down on 24th April 1991. An IBS, still in current use, was installed in 2008. All goods facilities were closed by 4th May 1970.

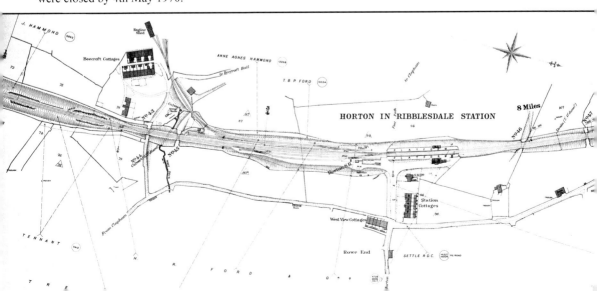

11. An unidentified Midland 4-4-0 on a local service pulls away from the station heading towards Settle and passing Horton box in September 1908. (John Alsop collection)

12. Class 158 no. 158845 is seen here on 4th November 2024 on a Leeds - Carlisle service passing under the new footbridge in the final stages of construction. (Mark Bartlett)

➜ *Inset: Taken on the same day a view of the new footbridge at the southern end of the station. Note the additional stairway on the downside that will take the Three Peaks Challenge footpath over the soon to be relaid siding to Horton quarry. (Mark Bartlett)*

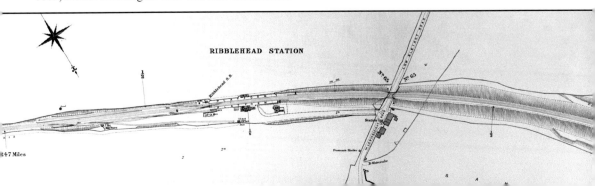

→ *Decorative station signage on the up platform. (ColourRail.com)*

HORTON-IN-RIBBLESDALE
ALTITUDE 850 FEET

CARLISLE ◄◄◄ 65 MILES

LONDON ►►► 242 MILES

WELCOME TO THE YORKSHIRE DALES

Selside Signal Box

The box was situated just north of the hamlet of Selside and opened on 16th June 1907, although opening dates of October 1876 and August 1877 have also been mentioned. It was closed on 30th November 1975 and was moved to Carnforth Steam Town. The box is worthy of particular mention because in WWII amid the ensuing manpower shortage local ladies took charge of the signal box.

The box was Grade II listed in February 1989 but in 1977 the heritage centre was closed, when the site became a railway operating centre and the box is now languishing and deteriorating sadly.

Selside Accident

In October 1968, at Selside just north of Horton-in-Ribblesdale station, a goods train from Preston en route to Carlisle collided with the rear of another goods train from Warrington to the same destination resulting in derailed wagons blocking the line for several days. There were two reported injured.

Ribblehead Quarry

Located to the south of Ribblehead station, the quarry was opened to provide stone for construction of the Settle & Carlisle Line. Later the stone was used in a variety of products. Quarrying operations ceased in 1907 and it wasn't until 1943 that limestone was extracted for agricultural purposes. Ballast from the adjacent quarry was still being loaded at Ribblehead until 1986 but it appears the quarry remained active some time after that. The northerly connection from the quarry siding to the mainline was resited in 1974, which necessitated removal of the down platform at the then closed Ribblehead station. The quarry had a variety of owner/operators over the years and the last, Hanson, handed the quarry to English Nature in 2000; it is now part of the Ingleborough National Nature Reserve. The sidings have been re-used for rail traffic where stone delivered by road from Ingleton quarry is loaded. Timber was also loaded at Ribblehead but only from August 2010 to 2012.

RIBBLEHEAD

V. Opened on 4th December 1876 as Batty Green, it was renamed Ribblehead not long after, on 1st May 1877. Like all other stations on the line, apart from earlier casualties and Settle and Appleby, the station was closed in 1970 after which the northbound platform was demolished as previously described. The station was re-opened on 16th July 1986 and a replacement down platform was constructed just to the south of the previous one on 28th May 1993. The station has been variously used as a chapel and meteorological station and it is now leased to the Settle & Carlisle Railway Trust that has painstakingly restored it to include a visitor centre with a shop and an exhibition about the Midland. The station signal box opened in December 1876, was replaced in July 1889, closed 17th August 1969 and later demolished.

RIBBLEHEAD STATION

13. Against the backdrop of a blue sky, Whernside, the Ribblehead viaduct and the Station Inn, BR Super Sprinter no. 158869 on 2H89 the 11.58 Carlisle - Leeds service is seen arriving at Ribblehead station on 9th January 2024. (Tom McAtee)

→   *The snow clearing crew are at the ready, although some do not look properly dressed. Presumably the warmth of the locomotive more than makes up for it. (John Alsop collection)*

↘   *BR HST set in Midland Pullman livery led by 43047 with 43046 tailing passes through Ribblehead station on Saturday 14th October 2023 with 1Z53 05.55 Eastleigh to Carlisle 'Settle & Carlisle Pullman'. The train is passing the staggered down platform and the siding to the stone and former timber loading facility. (Gordon Edgar)*

↓   14. Deeley & Johnson Compound MR class 1000 no. 1027 is on a down stopping train in 1909. (John Alsop collection)

15. In late snowfall BR class 158 no. 158758 on 2H85 08.24 Carlisle - Leeds service waits to move forward on 10th March 2023. The shot was taken from the staggered down platform. (Tom McAtee)

← *Crowds alight from the 'Yorkshire Dales Explorer' that had terminated at the staggered down platform on 8th June 2024. The BR class 156 Super Sprinters, headed by no. 156424, had travelled from Rochdale on the inaugural summer Saturday service that runs to Ribblehead via Manchester, Bolton and Clitheroe. (John Matthews)*

Ribblehead Viaduct

The Ribblehead viaduct was designed by the Midland Chief Engineer, John Crossley, and crosses Batty Moss after which it is sometimes referred. Work started in 1869 and up to 2,300 men (navvies) were employed in its construction and over 100 lost their lives in the process. The structure has 24 arches, although in the original plan 18 was deemed sufficient; it is 440 yards (400m) long and at its highest it sits 104ft (32m) above the valley floor. Every sixth pier is 50% thicker as a safeguard against the collapse of any of the other piers. The north end of the viaduct is 13ft (4m) higher than the southern end; a gradient of 1 in 100, which is consistent with the overall gradient of the Long Drag.

It is the longest structure on the line and there are two that exceed it in height, Crosby Garrett and Arten Gill. The viaduct is largely brick-built, some 1.5 million in all, and is faced with lime stone. The estimated cost of construction amounted to £343,000. The viaduct was unofficially opened to traffic on 6th September 1874 when a passenger train crossed on a single track hauled by a locomotive named *Diamond* and, following approval of the Board of Trade, the line was opened to freight traffic on 3rd August 1875 and passenger traffic on 1st May 1876. By 1980 the viaduct was in a state of disrepair and the cost of restoration, that included singling the track, amounted to about £100,000 and in 1989 a waterproof membrane was laid under the track. In the 1980s BR proposed closing the Settle & Carlisle line mentioning the cost of repairs to various structures would be prohibitive, which subsequently proved not to be the case. That said work continues on its wellbeing and ability to continue carrying freight. The viaduct was Grade II listed in 1988.

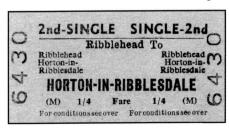

2nd-SINGLE   SINGLE-2nd
Ribblehead To
Ribblehead   Ribblehead
Horton-in-   Horton-in-
Ribblesdale   Ribblesdale
HORTON-IN-RIBBLESDALE
(M)   1/4   Fare   1/4   (M)
For conditions see over   For conditions see over

16. *The last post...*
Ribblehead Viaduct on 1st November 2004. In the foreground is the Station Inn. If one stands in either the Ladies or Gents at the Inn, both have a panoramic view of the viaduct so nothing is missed when needs must. (John Furnevel)

17. Ex-LMS Stanier Jubilee class 4-6-0 no. 45699 *Galatea* crosses Batty Moss (Ribblehead) viaduct, glimpsed from Gunnerfleet Farm, hauling the 1Z40 Broxbourne to Carlisle 'Cathedrals Express' charter on 5th March 2014.
(Gordon Edgar)

↓ 18. A pair of BR Type 5 class 56 Co-Co nos 56098, in BR blue large logo livery, and 56049, in Colas livery, on a Chirk timber train on 9th January 2024.
(Tom McAtee)

Blea Moor Sidings

It is bleak, isolated and almost inaccessible yet it is an important spot on the Settle & Carlisle line. It is at this point that freight trains from the Arcow, Ribblehead and in future Horton sidings that are booked to travel south come to reverse and take the up line. The first signal box at this location was opened on 2nd August 1875 and was replaced in 1892 and 1914; the last one on the up side was opened on 16th December 1941.

19. In stunning winter conditions and a snow-covered Whernside at 2,415ft (736m) dominating, ex-LMS Stanier Royal Scot class 4-6-0 no. 46115 *Scots Guardsman* passes Blea Moor signal box and sidings with the northbound 'Cumbrian Fellsman' on 7th February 2009. (Dick Manton)

Blea Moor Tunnel

At 1.494 miles (2.404km) Blea Moor tunnel is the longest on the Settle & Carlisle line being almost double the length of the second-longest, Rise Hill Tunnel. It took more than four years to construct and was completed in 1875 at a cost of £109,000. The line passes 500ft (152m) below Blea Moor and during construction seven shafts were sunk from above allowing greater flexibility in the use of manpower. Four of the shafts were filled-in and three remain to this day as an aid to ventilation.

This shot taken on 8th June 2021 shows the southernmost ventilator shaft of Blea Moor tunnel constructed in 1874. (Gordon Edgar)

20. An unidentified Midland 4-4-0 and train exit the southern portal of the tunnel in May 1908. (John Alsop collection)

Dent Head Viaduct

The viaduct in Dentdale stands just north of Blea Moor tunnel at milepost 251. Work started on it in 1869 but was often delayed due to heavy rainfall so it wasn't completed until 1875. The viaduct is 596ft (182m) long and stands 100ft (30m) at its highest point. The viaduct is recognisable by its 10 arches grouped into two sets of five with a larger pier in the centre and it is built of Blue Limestone that was quarried nearby. In January 1998 a High Marnham bound coal train derailed near Dent Head causing considerable damage to the track and an under bridge. There were no injuries and the cause was attributed to poor maintenance leading to renewal of all track on the line. In January 1999 a similar incident occurred at this location. In its efforts to close the line BR cited Dent Head viaduct along with others as decaying and unsafe; this claim was rebutted by an independent civil engineer, who declared it structurally sound. In 1999, Dent Head viaduct was Grade II listed.

21. A long distance view of Dent Head taken on 1st April 1989 as a pair of BR class 108 DMUs are seen crossing the viaduct. (ColourRail.com/ S.R. Lee)

2. Dent Head to Smardale Viaduct
17 Miles (27km)

The contract for this section amounting to £335,000 was awarded to Messrs Benton and Woodiwiss in November 1869. Up to 1,400 men were employed on this section. Work under contract no. 2 started immediately after Dent Head viaduct.

Dent Head Signal Box

22. Ex-LMS Hughes Crab 2-6-0 no. 42771 with a northbound freight is passing Dent Head signal box on 26th July 1962 having just crossed the viaduct. The original box was opened on the site in 1877 and was replaced in November 1898. The box closed on 11th April 1965 and was later demolished. (Roger Joanes)

Arten Gill Viaduct

Another designed by John Crossley; initial work started on the viaduct in May 1870 with construction completed in July 1875. Arten Gill viaduct has 11 arches, is 660ft (200m) long and at its highest point above ground is 117ft (36m), making it the second highest viaduct after Smardale. Typically it has two sets of widened piers to ensure structural integrity in case of partial collapse. Due to unstable ground conditions, some of the viaduct piers were sunk to 55ft (17m). It is constructed from a mix of sandstone and Dent marble; the latter being quarried locally. The viaduct crosses Artengill beck and, as with many place names, it can be written with one or two words.

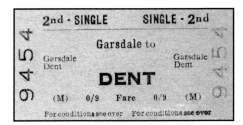

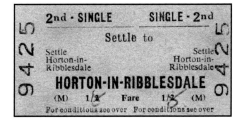

23. View from beneath the towering arches of Arten Gill viaduct, taken in June 2013. (Julian Thurgood)

24. BR Brush Traction class 60 no. 60021 is heading north over Arten Gill viaduct on 8th September 2004 with the 04.57 Drax - Kirkby Thore service. It comprised 16 FCA wagons loaded with containers of desulphogypsum (gypsum produced by the flue gas desulphurisation plant at Drax power station) for use in manufacturing plasterboard. It was the desulphogypsum traffic that brought freight back to the line in the early 1990s. (Paul Shannon)

DENT

VI. Situated between Blea Moor and Rise Hill tunnels, at 1,150 ft (351m) above sea level, Dent is the highest mainline station in England. It was opened on 6th August 1877 and closed during the BR cut backs on 4th May 1970; it was re-opened 14th July 1986. There is no footbridge at the station so passengers must cross to the up platform via a barrow crossing at the north end of the station that has led to a mandatory 30mph (48kmh) speed restriction for all through trains. Dent station is located near the hamlet of Cowgill but approximately 5 miles (8 km) from the village of Dent, famous for its annual Dentdale Music & Beer Festival, held in June. The signal box was opened on 6th August 1877 and its replacement on 9th August 1891. It finally closed on 28th January 1981 and burned down in September 1984. The goods facilities at the station were taken out of use on 1st October 1964. Another feature of the station are the remains of the wooden snow fences rising above the station on the up side. While the station was closed during the 1970s it was rented out to Barden School in Burnley as accommodation for pupils on outward bound courses.

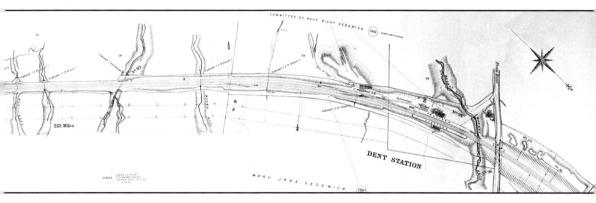

25. On a cold winter's day, with frost still on the sleepers at lunchtime, Large Logo class 47 no. 47503 is about to depart with the 10.42 Leeds - Carlisle service on 9th December 1987. (Martyn Hilbert)

The Staycation Express

The North Pennine Staycation Express, operated by Rail Charter Services Ltd, was a tourist train running three times a day between Skipton and Appleby from July through September 2020. It ran again in 2021 but through to Carlisle and until the end of October. The all first class stock was hired in from Locomotive Services Ltd (LSL) based at Crewe along with the 2 + 5 HST set used in 2021. Due to extraordinary trading conditions the Staycation service was suspended in 2022 with hopes that it would run again the following year. Sadly it was not to be, but there have been other summer services since then on the line. Lack of political support did not help the cause either, which must have been frustrating for the operator, as for example it had brought 20,000 new visitors into the area in 2020.

26. In this shot the Staycation Express is seen heading south on 12th August 2020 through Dent station. At the front is preserved BR English Electric Type 2 Bo-Bo no. D8107 (TOPS 20107) and at the rear preserved at Crewe is BR class 47 no. 47712 *Lady Diana Spencer* in BR Scotrail livery. Snow fences are visible in the background, as mentioned in Map VI on the previous page. (Tom McAtee)

27. During a very brief respite in the heavy rainfall throughout the day, the 15.09 Carlisle to Skipton Staycation Express service is seen passing through Dent station on 27th October 2021. At the front of the LSL-owned BR class 43 (HST set) is no. 43059 with 43058 at the rear. (Gordon Edgar)

Rise Hill Tunnel

Known also as Black Moss, Cowgill and Risehill tunnel, it is the second-longest on the line at 1,213yds (1,109m) but is only about half the length of Blea Moor tunnel. It lies beneath Black Moss and at its deepest point is 170ft (52m) below the surface. Work on the tunnel began in May 1870; again the idea of opening ventilation shafts was adopted with four teams descending and working outwards from each. Spoil was removed through two shafts and scattered around the site. Building work took four years to complete and the tunnel was opened officially on 2nd August 1875. The tunnel was some distance from civilisation and so workers were accommodated in a shanty town that was home to about 200 people. It was the highest of such camps along the line and suffered greatly due to heavy rainfall and bad winters; so much so that the contractor provided a better class of accommodation for the navvies. A memorial to those who worked on the tunnel or died during construction can be seen in Dent churchyard.

The tunnel runs between Dentdale and Garsdale but a diversion around Black Moss had been considered in order to avoid tunnelling but this would have added 8 miles (13km) to the journey. Rise Hill tunnel boasted two signal boxes one each at the north and south ends; they opened some time in early 1877 and both closed in April 1878 and were later demolished.

28. The south entrance to Rise Hill tunnel, taken on 7th July 1974. (Michael Ellis)

Garsdale Water Troughs

A mile (1.6km) after the tunnel were the Garsdale water troughs said to be the highest in the world. They were installed in 1907 where the line crosses Ling Gill and were just over a quarter of a mile (400m) in length; the site was chosen because the line was both relatively flat and straight, plus water was plentiful. A dam was constructed above the site of the troughs and water flowed into a tank house that fed them. The tank house held 43,000 imperial gallons (nearly 200,000 litres) and the troughs about 5,000 to 6,000 gallons each (23,000 to 27,000 litres) each. To stop the tank from freezing, a system of pipes with steam heating was used and this had to be manned on such occasions. A gang was also engaged in de-icing the water troughs; had the ice in the troughs expanded above rail level there was a danger of derailing a passing train. The troughs were removed in 1968 just prior to the end of steam on BR.

29. Seen from track level on 15th May 1965 is Black 5 no. 44711 with a mixed freight taking on water. On the left behind milepost 258 the water tank that fed the troughs can be seen.
(C. Weston/Kidderminster Railway Museum)

GARSDALE

VII. Opened as Hawes Junction on 1st August 1876; it was renamed Hawes Junction and Garsdale on 20th January 1900 and finally renamed Garsdale on 1st September 1932. During the BR run down of the line, the station was itself closed 4th May 1970 and reopened on 14th July 1986. The goods facilities were closed on 4th October 1965. Apart from the 16 cottages near the station erected for railway employees and a further eight close by the Moorcock Inn, there is little else in terms of habitation near the station but it served as a junction for the line to the market town of Hawes some 5 miles (8km) to the east. Compared with the days when the station was a busy junction facilities today are sparse. It is an unstaffed halt, although the signal box is manned, with waiting rooms on each platform and a toilet on the up platform. There is no link between the platforms other than using footpaths and lanes that run under the line north and south of the platforms. The waiting room of the northbound platform was used for church services; the ladies waiting room contained a library of 150 books and the stone base of the water tower was used as a village hall.

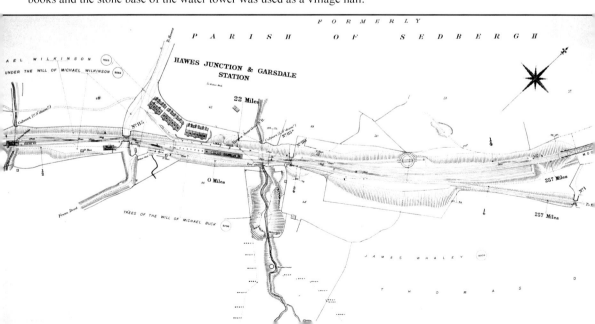

30. A busy Hawes Junction station, as it then was, around 1910 with a down Carlisle-bound service to the left and a Hawes branch train standing in the platform to the right. (John Alsop collection)

31. Passengers alight from a northbound 'DalesRail' service, provided by a BR MetCamm four-car class 101/2 DMU, on 2nd October 1976. Garsdale station had been closed since 1970 but, despite this, the DalesRail service was an early initiative to revive use of the line for passenger traffic. The venture was a success and led to several stations on the line being restored for seasonal use from May 1975 to accommodate the DalesRail services, although Garsdale did not reopen officially until 1986. (Roger Joanes)

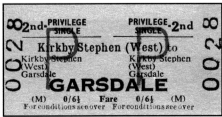

32. On the up platform is a life-size bronze statue of a border collie by Joel Walker, named Ruswarp, which was unveiled on 11th April 2009. His owner was Graham Nuttall a founding member of FoSCL the first group set up to save the line. In fact, Ruswarp even signed the initial petition to save the line with a paw print. In January 1990, Graham and his dog were walking in the Welsh hills and went missing. Graham's body wasn't found until 7th April and miraculously Ruswarp was still alive after 11 weeks standing guard over his deceased master. Sadly, Ruswarp died shortly after attending Graham's funeral. In this view, taken on 7th August 2021, Ruswarp is overseeing the long-overdue renovation of the station signal box. (Gordon Edgar)

33. Battling against a strong southwesterly wind and driving rain, Gresley Pacific no. 60103 *Flying Scotsman,* rebuilt as an A3 in 1947, whisks through Garsdale heading the 1Z62 15.44 Carlisle to Middlesbrough charter on 27th October 2021, which was steam-hauled to York. The Bobby of the recently renovated 1910-built MR Type 4 signal box waves and receives an acknowledgement from the fireman while taking a short break from what must have been an arduous shift for the crew members. The name 'Bobby' dates back to the days when railway policemen were responsible for the signalling of trains and they were so named after Sir Robert Peel, who created the Metropolitan Police Force. (Gordon Edgar)

Garsdale Turntable

The turntable was constructed in the late 1900s to turn banking and pilot engines based at the station. The turntable was driven solely by muscle power and given its high altitude, over 1,000ft (305m) above sea level, heavy winds and drifting snow in the pit could make it almost impossible to turn heavy locomotives. Railway folklore has it that winds were so strong on one occasion that an engine spun around on the turntable for hours until the sand, earth and ballast were shovelled into the pit to clog up the works. Folklore or not, it inspired Rev. W. Awdry of 'Thomas the Tank Engine' fame to write the story 'Tenders and Turntables' that appears in his book 'Troublesome Engines'. Back to reality: the strong winds not only made it hard to turn an engine but very difficult to stop with any degree of accuracy. To alleviate the problem, a protective stockade of sleepers was built around the turntable. The turntable fell out of use in the 1960s due to the demise of steam and, on 26th February 1989, key components were removed and taken to the Keighley and Worth Valley Railway where they were installed on the turntable at Keighley in 1990 and remain in operation to this day.

34. Ex-LNER Worsdell class D20 (formerly NER class R) 4-4-0 no. 62347 is seen in this undated picture of the protected turntable. Presumably this engine was being turned for the return journey towards Northallerton via Hawes. (Robert Humm collection)

Garsdale Signal Boxes

At one time, the remote station boasted three signal boxes. Hawes Junction South Box opened on 2nd August 1875, was replaced on 3rd July 1892 and closed on 10th July 1910 and later demolished. The North Box also opened on 2nd August 1875, was replaced on 16th August 1891 and also closed on 10th July 1910 and later demolished. The Hawes Junction Box was opened on 10th July 1910; renamed Garsdale Station SB on 1st September 1932. It was temporarily out of use between 1983 and the mid-1990s but is now in current use. It is one of two boxes on the line that are closed at night. The timber box with a Welsh slate roof was Grade II listed in 2013, which meant that, when the box was refurbished in 2021, Network Rail had to apply to the Yorkshire Dales National Park Authority in order to carry out the necessary repairs.

Dandry Mire Viaduct

Also known as Moorcock or Garsdale viaduct it was originally planned that the line would cross Dandry Mire by way of an embankment. Work started on the crossing in 1871 but over 250,000 cubic yards (190,000m³) was swallowed up by the bog below not helped by continual wet weather, which meant a change of plan and so work on constructing a viaduct instead began in 1873. Originally designed to have eight sandstone arches a further change led to a 12-arch viaduct being completed in September 1875. Piers for the pillars were dug 15ft (4.6m) into the ground and the arches were grouped so the fourth and eighth pillars were thicker to ensure the viaduct's integrity. It is 681ft (207m) long and 50ft (15m) at its highest above the valley floor. The viaduct is a prominent landmark at the head of Garsdale where rainfall and snowmelt are channelled into the River Eden, the River Rawthey and its tributary Clough River, which run into the Lune, and the River Ure that runs east to join the River Ouse and eventually the Humber. The viaduct was Grade II listed in June 1984.

35. Black 5 no. 44983 is seen heading north across the viaduct on 28th May 1966. Note the Zion chapel in the foreground. (ColourRail.com)

➜ *Railway contractors, Benton and Woodiwiss, provided a wooden structure near the railway for use as a school, reading room and chapel. Once railway construction work was completed and a permanent community was in residence, the Middleham Primitive Methodist Church raised funds for the permanent Zion chapel. The foundation stone was laid on 1st May 1876 to coincide with the opening of the line to passenger traffic and was completed for the inaugural services on 7th October 1876. The windows and doors were painted in MR colours. It is interesting to note that the chapel perpetuates the long forgotten name of 'Hawes Junction' as its location. In this shot, taken on 2nd April 1988, large logo class 47 no. 47578* Royal Society of Edinburgh *is heading past the chapel with the diverted 12.10 Glasgow-Euston train. (Noel Machell)*

Moorcock Tunnel

At just 98 yards (90m) Moorcock Tunnel is one of the shortest on the line and on a relatively sharp radius curve. It was excavated through a ridge of boulder clay and constructed between 1871 and 1875.

← 36. Leeds Holbeck-based ex-LMS Jubilee class 6P5F no. 45694 *Bellerophon*, with a down passenger service M931, emerges from the north end of Moorcock tunnel in the 1950s. (Cumbrian Railways Association, Mayor collection ref MAY016)

Lunds Viaduct

At 103 yards (94m) long and with five arches, the highest of which above the valley below is 60ft (18.3m), Lunds viaduct is one of the smaller structures on the line.

37. Lunds viaduct looking south after a light dusting of snow on 27th December 1984. (Michael Ellis)

38. Class 158 Super Sprinter no. 158758 heads 1E65 the 13.36 Carlisle - Leeds service on 8th August 2023 and is about to enter Moorcock tunnel. Just beyond the footbridge to the north is the scene of the Hawes Junction collision of 24th December 1910 - see overleaf. (Stephen Willetts)

Shotlock Hill Tunnel

At 106 yards (97m) Shotlock Hill tunnel is relatively short and was constructed between 1871 and 1875.

← *On 16th February 2017, Peppercorn class A1 no. 60163* Tornado *is heading northbound '1 ♥ S&C' rail tour on the Skipton-Appleby leg exiting the north portal. On the rear was Alstom class 67 Bo-Bo no. 67029 that provided electric train heating. This was one of 12 services operated by Northern in a week between Appleby and Skipton as part of celebrations to mark the reopening of the line after landslides near Armathwaite. (Gordon Edgar)*

Hawes Junction Rail Crash (at Ais Gill Moor)

On 24th December 1910, a Scotland-bound express ran into two banking engines returning light to Carlisle some 3 miles (4.8km) north of Garsdale station at Ais Gill Moor. Two banking engines were waiting for the road at Garsdale station but, unwittingly, the busy Garsdale signalman cleared the road not for the seemingly forgotten two light engines but the oncoming express. The express hit the light engines just north of the Lunds viaduct near the Ais Gill summit with the inevitable consequences and devastation. There were 12 fatalities and 17 injured. The subsequent Board of Trade accident report recommended the installation of track circuits interlocked with signals that would have prevented the accident and the MR complied accordingly with immediate effect.

← *The disaster at Ais Gill Moor on 24th December 1910. (John Alsop collection)*

Ais Gill Summit

Ais Gill summit is the highest point on the line at 1,169ft (356m) above sea level. It stands at the head of the Mallerstang Valley just before the present day boundary between Cumbria and North Yorkshire. Over 1,000ft (305m) higher in the moorlands above the Mallerstang Valley, two streams join to form Hell Gill Beck and after flowing over the spectacular Hellgill Force waterfall, the highest on the River Eden, it then proceeds sedately as the River Eden down the Mallerstang valley towards Kirkby Stephen; thereafter, the railway roughly follows the course of the river towards Carlisle. Ais Gill signal box was opened on 2nd August 1875, replaced on 24th June 1900 and closed on 28th January 1981; an IBS was installed in 2009 and is currently in use. The box was dismantled and relocated to the Midland Railway Centre at Butterley during 1982-83.

The sign marking the high point of the line. (ColourRail.com)

39. Midland class 801 4-4-0 no. 2606 passes the Ais Gill signal box at the highest point on the line. The passing loops were installed originally for detached banking engines to muster before returning to Hawes Junction for their next assignment. (John Alsop collection)

40. On 28th November 1964 an unidentified Carlisle-bound passenger service is seen passing Ais Gill box at the summit. (ColourRail.com/R.K. Green)

L. M. & S. R.

FOR CONDITIONS SEE BACK

HawesJunc&Garsdale to
SETTLE

THIRD
CLASS   3020 (S)   FARE 2 7
           SETTLE

Ais Gill Accident

In September 1913, a London-bound passenger train was struggling to reach the Ais Gill Summit; a problem not uncommon with the relatively small Midland engines. The first train stopped quite close to the site of the 1910 accident in order to build up a head of steam and was hit by the second train. There were 16 fatalities and 38 injured. The inquiry identified a number of causes of the accident and apportioned blame accordingly. It also made recommendations to avoid such a disaster happening again, including introduction of the nascent Automatic Train Control.

➔ *The aftermath of the disaster that occurred on 2nd September 1913. (John Alsop collection)*

Ais Gill Viaduct

A few miles south of Birkett Tunnel and Kirkby Stephen sits Ais Gill Viaduct, which at 87 yds (80m) long and 75ft (23m) high, with four arches, is relatively small.

41. Large logo class 47 no. 47439 heads south over Ais Gill viaduct with a diverted WCML train on 2nd April 1988. Looking at the coaching stock it is most likely to have been a diverted Glasgow - Euston service. (Noel Machell)

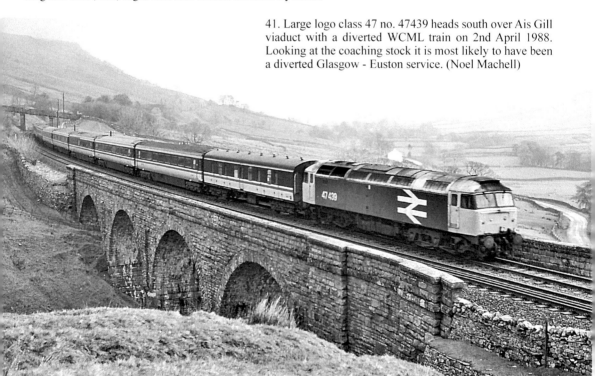

42. The sheer bulk of Wild Boar Fell at 2,323 ft (708m) dwarfs Stanier's Royal Scot class 4-6-0 no. 46115 *Scots Guardsman* as it approaches Ais Gill viaduct heading 'The Settle-Carlisle Railway Development Company's 30th Anniversary' charter, 1Z70 the 08.24 Carlisle - York service on 17th September 2022. (Gordon Edgar)

Mallerstang Signal Box

The box opened on 2nd August 1875; it was replaced on 9th September 1894 and finally closed on 31st August 1969. An IBS was installed in 2009 and is still in use. After closure the box was used by Permanent Way staff and on one occasion a coat was left by the stove; it caught fire and, as a consequence, the box was destroyed.

← *Photograph of Mallerstang signal box taken in October 1921. (John Alsop collection)*

Birkett Tunnel

The tunnel, which is 424yds (388m) long and runs more or less north-south, was completed in December 1875.

43. Crewe-based class 47s in restored two-tone green livery D1935 (TOPS 47805) *Roger Hosking MA 1925 - 2013* and D1924 (TOPS 47810) *Crewe Diesel Depot* head down the grade having exited Birkett tunnel heading towards Kirkby Stephen and Appleby with 1Z47 the 08.32 Uttoxeter-Appleby 'Settle & Carlisle Circular' charter at Greengate on 28th January 2023. (Gordon Edgar)

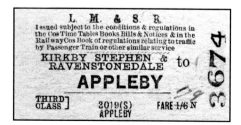

KIRKBY STEPHEN

VIII. Opened on the 1st May 1876 as Kirkby Stephen, the name was changed to Kirkby Stephen and Ravenstonedale on 1st October 1900. It was again renamed Kirkby Stephen West on 8th June 1953 and finally took the name Kirkby Stephen on 6th May 1968 after the other station in the town Kirkby Stephen East was closed to passengers in 1962. The station closed in 1970 as BR attempted to close the line but was re-opened after prolonged campaigning on 14th July 1986. Kirkby Station East re-opened to traffic as the base of the Stainmore Railway Company in August 2011 on the former North Eastern Railway's Stainmore and Eden Valley lines. Kirkby Stephen station is more than 1¼ miles (2 km) from the town and over 150ft (46m) above it at Midland Hill. This was in keeping with the MR's desire to keep gradients at or below 1 in 100. The station is leased from Network Rail by the Settle and Carlisle Railway Trust that embarked on a programme of comprehensive restoration, including the provision of holiday accommodation. The former goods shed is now privately owned and still in use; goods facilities were withdrawn on 28th September 1964. The original signal box opened on 2nd August 1875 and was replaced 6th May 1894 and later renamed Kirkby Stephen West SB in June 1953. A new replacement box was opened in October 1974 making extensive use of parts moved from Kendal signal box, which closed on 19th April 1973. Kirkby Stephen signal box is still currently in use. Garsdale to Kirkby Stephen is the longest section on the line at 9½ miles (15.3km) without a station.

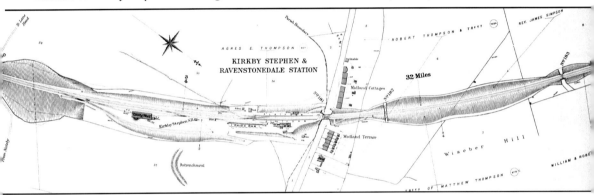

44. BR Riddles Standard class 9F 2-10-0 no. 92052 seen passing Kirkby Stephen goods shed in 1964. It is returning from Widnes with empty anhydrite wagons bound for the Long Meg sidings.
(Peter Fidczuk collection)

→ 45. Looking north in the late 1950s/early 1960s, Black 5 no. 45259 is standing in the station with the 08.05 ex-Carlisle.
(Robert Humm collection)

↘ 46. Seen alongside the 1894 signal box, in the summer of 1974, is the replacement box, which was commissioned in October of that year. Both are mentioned on the previous page.
(Alan Crispin Mayor collection courtesy of Rob Daniels)

↓ 47. Royal Scot no. 46115 *Scots Guardsman* seen on 13th March 2017 with the southbound 'Cumbrian Mountain Express'; it seems unusual to see the station virtually deserted when there is steam on the line and on such a fine day. The station building is one of the largest designs of the three variants on the line, as evidenced by the four chimney stacks.
(Peter van Campenhout)

Smardale Viaduct

Just north of Kirkby Stephen the Smardale Viaduct is the highest on the line at 131ft (40m). It is 237yds (217m) long featuring 12 arches and is constructed entirely of limestone. It was Grade II listed in 1976. It passes over Scandal Beck that runs through Smardale Gill, which is a nature reserve under the care of Cumbria Wildlife Trust. The old North Eastern Railway line, formerly the South Durham and Lancashire Union railway, from Darlington to Tebay also passed under this viaduct and about a mile south stands the preserved Old Smardale viaduct that also crosses Scandal Beck.

48. The Southbound Cumbrian Mountain Express hauled by Black 5 no. 5407 plus ETHEL for steam heating crossing Smardale viaduct on 13th January 1990. (Dick Manton)

49. General Electric class 70 Co-Co no. 70807 crossing Smardale Viaduct on the 09.24 Mountsorrel - Carlisle service with a loaded ballast train for Network Rail on 17th April 2019. (Steve Sienkiewicz)

3. Crosby Garrett Tunnel to New Biggin
15 Miles (24km)

The contract for this section amounting to approximately £279,000 was awarded to Joseph Fairbanks in March 1870 and up to 1,500 men were employed on this section of the line.

Crosby Garrett Tunnel

At 181yds (166 m) long) Crosby Garrett Tunnel is relatively short. Built between 1873 and 1875 the alternative to a tunnel at this point would have either been a deep cutting or for the line to follow the contours, which would have added miles to the journey north.

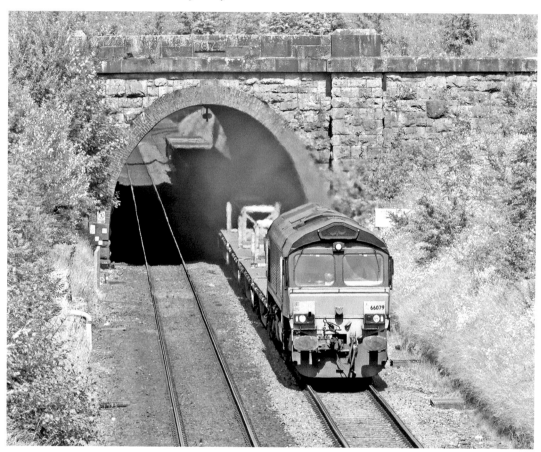

50. DB Schenker class 66 no. 66079 *James Nightall GC* emerges from the 181 yard-long Crosby Garrett tunnel, heading the 6L41 Carlisle Yard to Hellifield Engineer's working on 28th July 2012. (Gordon Edgar)

Crosby Garrett Accident

On 15th January 1999 a landslip caused a Carlisle-bound Sprinter to derail near Crosby Garrett Tunnel but the quick thinking driver managed to warn the driver of an up heavy coal train hauled by a Brush class 60 to slow sufficiently enough to avoid a major accident, although it did push the Sprinter about 300ft (91.4m) into the tunnel. There were no fatalities and only minor injuries.

Crosby Garrett Viaduct

A relatively small viaduct that passes through the village of that name is 110yds (110m) long, 55ft (17m) high comprising six arches and construction took place between 1869 and 1875. It was Grade II listed on 9th March 1984.

51. With Driver Gordon Hodgson at the regulator, Gresley 'K4' 2-6-0 no. 61994 *The Great Marquess* heads 1Z52, the 08.07 Lancaster to Carlisle 'Fellsman' charter, across Crosby Garrett viaduct on 29th August 2012. (Gordon Edgar)

CROSBY GARRETT

IX. The station was almost immediately to the north of the viaduct of the same name. The former opened on 1st May 1876 and closed as long ago as 5th October 1952. The platforms were set into the cutting and, to provide space, hefty retaining walls were required. These remain in situ so can be seen from passing trains. The station master's house exists as a private dwelling near the overbridge. The station signal box was opened on 2nd August 1875, replaced on 16th April 1899 and closed on 12th April 1965; it was later demolished. An IBS was installed in 2009 and is currently in use. The goods yard closed for business on 6th October 1962.

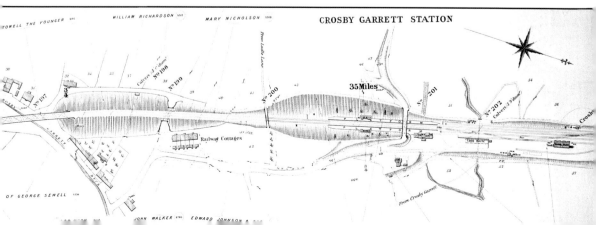

L.M. & S.R. For conditions see Back
PRIVILEGE TICKET
Valid 7 days
Third Class Single

L.M. & S.R. For conditions see Back
PRIVILEGE TICKET
Valid 7 days
Third Class Single

Crosby Garrett
Crosby Garrett   To

KIRKBY STEPHEN (LM)
KirkbyStephen   KirkyStephen

×/2. Z   FARE   ×/2. Z

375   375

52. Two railway men await the oncoming train heading south. This view looking north was taken beyond where the overbridge crossed the station.
(John Alsop collection)

← *The box and staff photographed in around 1900.*
(Robert Humm Collection)

Griseburn Viaduct

Built between 1873 and 1875, the viaduct reputedly marks the halfway point of the line. It has seven arches, is 142 yds (130m) long and 74ft (22.6m) high.

53. BR class 47 no. 47434 with a southbound passenger is working on 3rd March 1984 with snow on the Appleby fells in the background. As the photographer mentioned, this is one of the least photographed viaducts on the line. Plus by now it is likely that the viaduct is obscured by trees. (David Price)

Griseburn Ballast Sidings

Stone was quarried here for use as ballast on the railway from the late 19th century to the early 20th. Ballast wagons were stabled here ready for use as necessary. The sidings were controlled by a signal box that opened on 10th December 1905 but it is not clear when the sidings were taken out of use. The box was closed on 28th January 1981 and later demolished.

Helm Tunnel

Soon after, the line passes through Helm tunnel, which is relatively long at 571yds (522m).

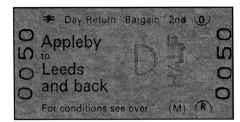

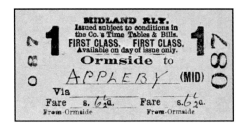

ORMSIDE

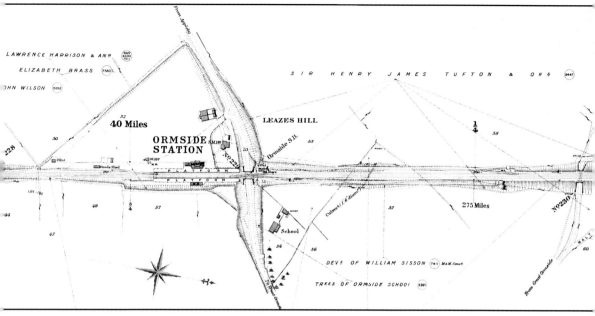

X. Situated just south of Appleby and just over 33 miles (53km) from Carlisle, original plans had suggested a station at Great Asby but objections from local landowners had the site relocated to near Great Ormside. The station opened on 1st May 1876 and closed on 2nd June 1952 as was the goods facility. Thereafter the platforms were demolished but the station building remains as a residential education centre for children from Knowsley and the northwest to engage in outdoor activities and education. Ormside station signal box was opened in 1876 and was replaced on 11th August 1907. It was closed on 8th March 1960 and later demolished; an IBS was installed in 2009 and is currently in use.

54. A view of Ormside station looking south in 1905. (John Alsop collection)

Ormside Viaduct

Built between 1870 and 1875 the viaduct has 10 arches, is 200yds (183m) long and 90ft (27.4m) high. The viaduct crosses the River Eden that is quite substantial at this point.

55. In this undated shot, an ex-LMS 0-6-0 is hauling a mixed freight across the viaduct. (John Alsop collection)

56. The sheep scatter as Coronation Class no. 46233 *Duchess of Sutherland* makes a fine sight storming across Ormside viaduct and getting into her stride after the Appleby water stop. The *Duchess* is heading 1Z87, the 14.40 Carlisle to London Euston 'Winter Cumbrian Mountain Express', on 31st January 2015. It was built in 1938 but not streamlined after just over 25 years of service, before retirement in 1964. *Duchess of Sutherland* ran 1,650,000 miles (2,660,000km), the second highest mileage by any member of the class. (Gordon Edgar)

APPLEBY

XI. Along with Settle, Appleby station remained open for business after BR had closed all other open stations on the line in May 1970. Opened as Appleby on 1st May 1876, it was renamed Appleby West on 1st September 1952 to avoid confusion with the other station in the town and reverted to Appleby on 6th May 1968, although Appleby East had closed some time before in 1962. Stations along the line are built of local stone from nearby quarries with the exception of Appleby which is brick-built. Beyond the station to the north are various engineering sidings that previously connected to the former NER line, now the Eden Valley Railway, which was used by the Ministry of Defence to access the local firing ranges at Warcop until the NER was closed to freight traffic in the 1980s. The rails at the junction from Appleby with the EVR are still in place but heavily overgrown. Over the years Appleby boasted four signal boxes: Appleby Dairy Sidings appears to have been closed in 1931; Appleby South Junction opened on 2nd August 1875, closed on 26th October 1886 and was demolished. Next was Appleby Station box, opened in 1876 and replaced on 26th October 1886; renamed Appleby West in 1951 it closed on 24th October 1973, was demolished and replaced with a ground frame to the former NER line. Finally, Appleby North Junction box was opened on 2nd August 1876; it was replaced on 26th October 1890 and destroyed by fire on 4th June 1951. Its replacement was erected 120yds (110m) further north in 1951 on the up side and is currently in use. Both the main station building and the footbridge, which was moved there from Mansfield station in 1901, are Grade II listed. The town is host to the Appleby Horse Fair, an annual gathering of roughly 10,000 Romani people and travellers held in the town each year in early June.

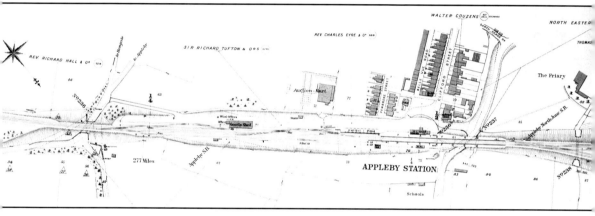

57. Midland Compound class 4-4-0 no. 2633 is taking on water on 3rd August 1906. (John Alsop collection)

58. In this undated shot ex-LMS Stanier class 8F 2-8-0 no. 48774 is heading a northbound mineral train through the station. (Robert Humm collection)

59. Taken from the footbridge, BR class 108 DMU, vehicle nos 56247 and 54247, in retro green livery heading for Carlisle is drawing into the station on 12th August 1986. The chimney and buildings of the Appleby Dairy complex can be seen in the background. (ColourRail.com/R. Siviter)

60. All the Virgin Super Voyagers were named after explorers, discoverers and voyagers; seen here is class 221 Super Voyager no. 221120 *Michael Palin*, which was named at Sheffield Midland on the 28th August 2002 by the TV personality himself. After a trip around Sheffield, it later took railway journalists and photographers to Carlisle to commence their annual visit organised by Virgin Trains and ScotRail. After dropping the party at Carlisle, the train returned south via the WCML. (D.A. Lovett)

61. A busy scene just beyond Appleby station on 9th September 2020. To the left is class 158 Super Sprinter no. 158872 given a clear road to Langwathby. In the centre is the North Box and to the right the 'Staycation Express' is stabled awaiting its return to Skipton. It will be headed by BR class 37 Co-Co no. D6851. It was renumbered 37151 in October 1973 then was rebuilt and renumbered 37667 in June 1987. It carried the name *Wensleydale* from October 1988 until December 1990, then *Merehead Quarry Centenary* from May 1997 until January 2001 and resides with Locomotive Services Limited at Crewe. On the rear, hidden from view, was class 47 no. 47712 *Lady Diana Spencer*. (John Matthews)

The Right Reverend Eric Treacy MBE, LL.D

A name familiar to many railway enthusiasts, Eric Treacy was ordained as a deacon in 1932 and devoted his life to the church; after a long and distinguished service to the church he was appointed Bishop of Wakefield in 1968 a post he held until retirement in 1976. His other great passion was railway photography to the extent that he amassed some 12,000 photos that are now held by the National Railway Museum; he also published a significant number of books about railways. On 13th May 1978 he suffered a heart attack on Appleby station while waiting presumably to photograph the 'Western Border Venturer' railtour headed by BR Standard Class 9F 2-10-0 no. 92220 *Evening Star*. On 30th September 1978 a service was held at Appleby station in memory of the 'Railway Bishop'. A slate plaque marking the occasion and his memory is exhibited on the main station building. In 1979 a Black 5 no. 45248 was named *Eric Treacy* and is preserved on the North Yorkshire Moors Railway. *Evening Star* was the last steam locomotive to be built by BR and was the only one of the class to be named and turned out in BR green. After stints on various heritage railways and on display at Swindon works it finally became a static exhibit at the NRM.

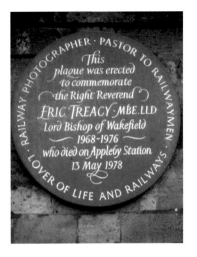

Memorial Service
for the Late, Right Reverend
Eric Treacy, M.B.E., LL.D.
Former Lord Bishop of Wakefield,
the 'Railway Bishop'
on Saturday 30 September 1978
at Appleby Station.

↑ 62. There was a large turn-out for Eric Treacy's memorial service on 30th September 1978 with *Evening Star* in the background at the head of the special.
(Tom Heavyside)

← *Order of Service.*
(Tom Heavyside)

↑*(top) This shot of the commemorative plaque was taken on 22nd November 1980 during a stop at Appleby while travelling on the 'Cumbrian Mountain Express' behind ex-LNER Gresley pacific no. 4498 (BR 60007) Sir Nigel Gresley. (Colin Kirkwood)*

Long Marton Viaduct

The viaduct has five arches is 60ft (18.3m) high and 180yds (165m) long and is built of red sandstone, quarried at nearby Dufton Hill.

63. Class 47 no. 47583 *County of Hertfordshire,* in Network South East livery, is in charge of the 12.37 Carlisle - Leeds service on 23rd April 1988. D1767 entered traffic in 1964 and sported various liveries and numbers while in service and finally no. 47734 *Crewe Diesel Depot Quality Approved.* On 28th September 2002 it had the distinction of piloting no. 47703 *Saint Mungo* on the First Great Western 15.40 service from Paignton to Paddington, the last regular locomotive hauled InterCity passenger service in the UK. (Peter Fitton)

LONG MARTON

XII. The station opened on 1st May 1876 and closed on 4th May 1970 as part of BR's plans to close the line but, unlike some other stations, it never re-opened. The main buildings were located on the up platform and have since been converted into private houses/holiday homes. Both platforms were demolished. The goods facility was closed on 6th April 1964. The signal box just south of the station, almost opposite the goods shed, was opened on 2nd August 1875, replaced in 1890, closed on 22nd March 1970 and later demolished.

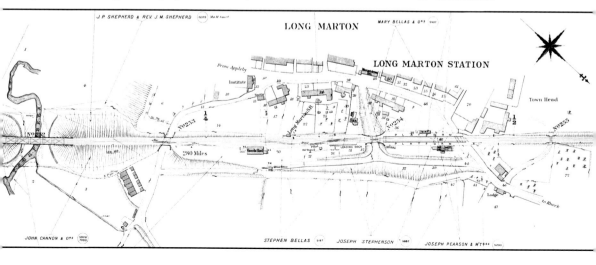

64. Taken some time in 1925, it looks like the station staff are waiting for a down train to arrive or pass through judging by the signal aspect. (John Alsop collection)

→ *Long Marton signal box seen on 29th June 1969 less than a year before it closed. With closure, transfer of control of McGhies ground frame was transferred to Appleby North box. (Robert Humm collection)*

Gypsum Mining and Plasterboard Production

Between Long Marton and New Biggin stations the area both east and west of the line was known for gypsum and barytes mining, along with the manufacture of products such as decorators plaster and plasterboard. The mining and manufacturing facilities required rail sidings for the various operations. Immediately south of Long Marton station, between bridges nos 253 and 254, was McGhie's sidings with an additional dedicated siding that served the nearby Silverband mine where processed barytes was transported from there to the siding by a ropeway. The sidings were closed and track lifted by September 1963. A little further north at Milepost 281¾ was the Gotham Co Ltd siding where the mined gypsum was transported to the railhead via a tramway; there is no date as and when the siding was taken out of use and lifted. Further north at MP 282 was the siding that served the McGhie Co Ltd Thistle Alabaster works. In 1935 these two companies were acquired by British Gypsum and in subsequent years extended the 'Thistle' sidings to more or less what can be seen today. Gypsum is still mined in the area. The name 'Thistle' remains as a brand of British Gypsum plaster as any decorators among you will know.

65. Andrew Barclay 0-4-0ST *Ken Boazman*, named after one of the company directors, works No. 2343 built in 1953 was provided new to British Gypsum. It is seen shorn of its nameplates raising steam in the early 1960s. The works are connected to the mainline and still receive product by rail but no longer use internal shunting locomotives as the product is delivered in containers. This locomotive is now preserved at the Ribble Steam Railway and is named *British Gypsum*. (Gordon Edgar)

66. BR class 60 Co-Co no. 60015 *Bow Fell*, in Loadhaul livery, stands in the unloading spur at the Kirkby Thore British Gypsum works on 4th April 2002. In this shot, empty containers are being reloaded on to the flat beds. From early October 2024 gypsum traffic to and from Teesside is routed via Carlisle and the Tyne Valley line. (Paul Shannon)

↓ 67. Northern's class 158 no. 158754 passes Kirkby Thore signal box and the British Gypsum works on 6th August 2024 with 2H90 the 13.18 Leeds - Carlisle service. (John Mahon)

NEW BIGGIN

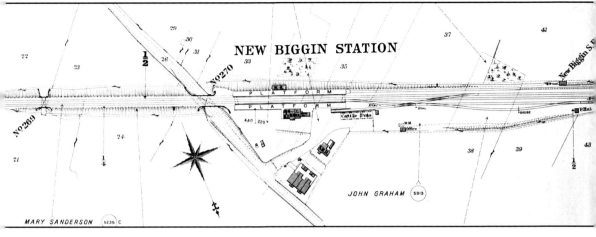

XIII. This station, which is also known as 'Newbiggin', opened on 1st May 1876 and closed on 4th May 1970 when BR withdrew local services on the line and, like the preceding station, it never re-opened. The buildings on the down platform survive as a private house but the platforms have since been demolished. The goods yard was closed on 7th November 1966. The signal box was located on the downside just to the north of the platforms and freight sidings. It opened on 2nd August 1875, was replaced on 12th July 1890 and closed on 16th December 1973 and later demolished.

68. New Biggin circa 1960 looking north towards Culgaith. The imposing bridge in the background carries a farmer's track over the line and is about a third of the distance to Culgaith.
(Lens of Sutton Association)

← *New Biggin station still survives as a private home. (ColourRail.com)*

4. Crowdundle Viaduct to Petteril Bridge
24 Miles (38.6km)

The contract for this section was awarded to Messrs Eckersley and Bayliss in April 1870 for £330,000 and up to 1,600 men were employed. Beyond Petteril Bridge the shared line into Carlisle was constructed by the North Eastern Railway.

Crowdundle Viaduct

Built in 1873 with four arches, 50ft (15m) high and 86yds (78.6m) long the viaduct crosses the Crowdundle Beck, a tributary of the River Eden. The Beck marked the pre-1974 county boundary between Cumberland and Westmorland.

69. Resplendent in its red livery preserved ex-LMS Jubilee class 5690 (BR 45690) *Leander* leaves a hazy trail of exhaust as it passes over Crowdundle viaduct near Culgaith with a southbound special on 26th April 1980. (Noel Machell)

CULGAITH

XIV. Culgaith station is only 1½ miles (2.4km) north of New Biggin station - the shortest distance between stations anywhere on the line between Leeds and Carlisle. Opened on 1st April 1880 it closed on 4th May 1970 when local stopping services were withdrawn by BR. Being built some four years after other stations on the line, the style is slightly different even though the same architect, John Holloway Sanders, was involved. The goods yard was taken out of use on 4th January 1965. The signal box opened in January 1880, was reframed on 20th September 1896 and a replacement opened on 4th October 1908. The box is still in use and controls the first of only two level crossings on the line; the other being at Low House just north of Armathwaite.

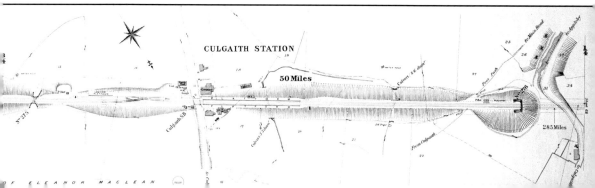

CULGAITH STATION

50 Miles

28½ Miles

70. An unidentified BR Cravens class 113 DMU is seen departing for New Biggin in 1966. The entrance to Culgaith tunnel can be seen to the north of the train. (Peter Fidczuk collection)

71. BR Brush Traction class 31 A1A-A1A no. 31469, with a rake of Mark 2 coaches, is heading south with a local service on 29th July 1990. By then the station had been closed for over 20 years. (ColourRail.com/R. Siviter)

Culgaith and Waste Bank Tunnels

Culgaith and Waste Bank tunnels are 660yds (604m) and 164yds (150m) long, respectively. In the case of Culgaith tunnel the original plan was to have a cutting at this point but that was abandoned in favour of boring a tunnel through the sandstone. On 6th March 1930, a local stopping train departed from Culgaith station in defiance of the signal and collided with an engineer's train that was unloading ballast in Waste Bank Tunnel. There were two fatalities and 35 injured.

Staingill Signal Box

Between the northern exit of Waste Bank tunnel and Langwathby station, Staingill signal box opened on 2nd August 1875 and closed 1879-80 and was later demolished.

LANGWATHBY

XV. Opened on 1st May 1876 as Longwathby, on the 1st of October that year the name was changed to Langwathby. It was closed by BR on 4th May 1970 when local stopping services were withdrawn and reopened on 14th July 1986. The Great North Air Ambulance, Cumbria base, is located close by the station and in July, since 2004, the village has held an annual scarecrow festival. There were fairly extensive sidings south of the station, which is where the signal box is located that were closed on 6th July 1964. The box opened on 2nd August 1875 as Longwathby and subsequently changed to Langwathby. The box was replaced on 5th July 1903 and closed on 27th October 1968 and later demolished. The sidings have been lifted but the goods shed remains and sits in what is now a chicken farm.

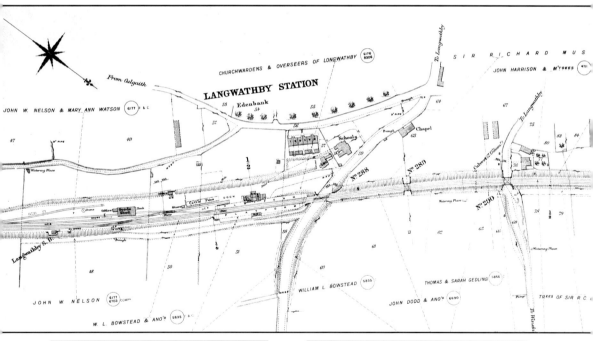

72. A very busy Langwathby Station is seen around 1900. (Lens of Sutton Association)

73. Ex-LMS Fowler class 4F 0-6-0 no. 44346 heads north in this undated shot with what looks like a rake of mainly mineral wagons. (ColourRail.com /R Tibbits)

74. In this undated shot class 156 Sprinter no. 156438 is departing on a southbound service in Northern blue livery with a green letter 'N' applied at one end. A number of units were painted in these colours between 1999 and 2001 and were later repainted in the current Northern colours when the Arriva franchise came to an end. The destination indicator on the rear vehicle is displaying 'York'; presumably it would have been changed if the unit made the return journey. (ColourRail.com)

Little Salkeld Viaduct

The viaduct sometimes referred to as Dodds Mill viaduct crosses Briggle Beck just to the south of the site of Little Salkeld station. It has seven arches, is 60ft (18m) high and 134yds (122.5m) long. The viaduct was Grade II listed on 9th March 1984.

75. A view of the viaduct taken from the nearby road on 1st June 2016. (Cumbrian Railways Association, Don Jary collection ref BS-AAF450)

LITTLE SALKELD

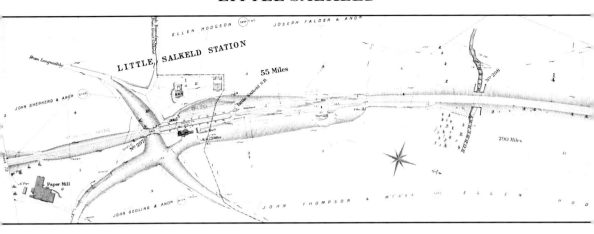

XVI. Little Salkeld opened on 1st May 1876 and closed on 4th May 1970 as it lost the local stopping service. The platforms remain in place and the station building is now a private house. The goods facilities closed on 6th July 1964. The signal box that stood at the north end of the down platform opened on 2nd August 1875, was replaced on 13th August 1899 and closed on 6th July 1964 and was later demolished.

➔ *A newly painted box shown in this undated shot was accompanied by a colour light starter signal and, to the right, an oil store or lamp room. (Robert Humm collection)*

76. An undated shot of the station looking south. It would appear that the station had been closed by the time this shot was taken. In the background is Thompsons paper mill that was transferred to Little Salkeld in 1900. (ColourRail.com/P. Bloxham)

Little Salkeld Accident

In January 1918 the Little Salkeld rail accident occurred just before footbridge no. 300, between Little Salkeld and Lazonby stations. A rapid thaw caused a landslip into which a London - Glasgow express ploughed, at between 50-60mph (80-97kph). There were seven fatalities and 46 injured.

Two cranes are seen lifting a 54ft (16.5m) MG&SW clerestory coach following the crash into the landslip on 19th January 1918. The River Eden can be seen beyond the landslip. (John Alsop collection)

Long Meg Mine

In 1885, the Long Meg Mine was opened by the Long Meg Plaster Co Ltd and was connected to the MR in 1886; it was located a couple of miles to the north of Langwathby station, directly adjacent to the Eden Lacy viaduct, where the line crosses the River Eden. Under a succession of owners, the mine was closed by 1915 and re-opened in 1922 for the extraction of anhydrite, which is used as a drying agent in plaster and cement. It was also a raw material in the production of sulphuric acid.

The mine secured a 20 year contract from 1954 to supply the United Sulphuric Acid Corporation of Widnes with 2500 tons of anhydrite a week for 20 years. The mine was purchased by what became British Gypsum who closed the mine in 1976. During the latter days of steam, anhydrite trains to Widnes ran from the sidings, typically hauled by BR Standard 9F 2-10-0s.

The Long Meg signal box opened in 1896 when shipments from the mine started. It was subsequently closed and replaced by a ground frame on 13th March 1915 until a new box opened on 3rd July 1955 that closed in 1973 and has been left to decay.

77. This shot of the extensive Long Meg sidings was taken from a passing train on 30th June 1963. To service this traffic a seven siding yard was installed and BR provided a fleet of dedicated hopper wagons, as seen in the photograph, which formed the consists of the famous BR Standard 9F 2-10-0 hauled trains on the S&C. These hoppers are seen in the lefthand most siding. (Peter Fidczuk collection)

78. This picture not only shows the Andrew Barclay shunter going about its business but is set against a stunning backdrop of the Eden Lacy viaduct. The 1968 Kilmarnock-built locomotive (works no. 552) *FGF,* named after a company director F. G. Flood, started life as a Barclay demonstration loco before being delivered to British Gypsum's Cocklakes Works on 29th July 1969, which was connected to the line at Howe & Co sidings, Cumwhinton. It was soon transferred to Long Meg Mine where it continued to make up trains for despatching anhydrite until the works closed and traffic ceased in January 1976. In September 1976 it was again transferred to the Thistle works at Kirkby Thore and on 16th November 1982 it was transferred to the Tanfield Railway and, since 2011, it has been in the care of the Bo'ness & Kinneil Railway after being donated by British Gypsum. (Gordon Edgar)

Eden Lacy Viaduct

Construction was completed in 1875. This seven arch viaduct is 137yds (125m) long and 60ft (18m) high and built of local sandstone. Some referred to it as the Long Meg viaduct after the nearby mine (see picture no. 78)

Lazonby Ballast Sidings Signal Box

The box opened by August 1877 and closed by February 1879 and was later demolished.

Lazonby Tunnel

A little further north, just short of Lazonby station, is the 99yds (91m)-long tunnel.

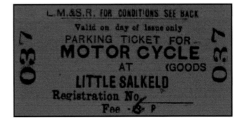

LAZONBY & KIRKOSWALD

XVII. Opened on 1st May 1876 as Lazonby, it was renamed Lazonby & Kirkoswald on 22nd July 1895. It was closed, like all other stations on the line bar two, on 4th May 1970 and re-opened on 14th July 1986. The buildings survived closure and the station was host to DalesRail excursions during this period. The goods yard was closed for business on 2nd November 1964. The station serves the villages of Kirkoswald, Lazonby and Great Salkeld. The signal box was opened on 2nd August 1875, replaced on 21st July 1895 and closed on 12th April 1965 and later demolished. An IBS was installed in 2008 and is currently in use.

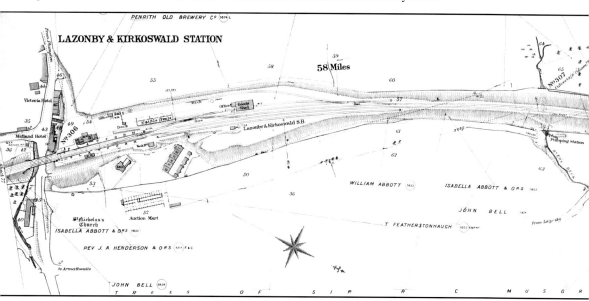

79. Looking south around 1960, we note the cattle dock and the Pooley Weighing Machine van in the end dock road. This van was converted from an ex-LNWR covered carriage truck. (Lens of Sutton Association)

80. Class 25 D5209 (TOPS 25059) heads south with 5M27 the regular Larber - Wallerscote soda ash empties on 24th August 1968; a service that continued until the early 1990s. The timetable for 1968 shows that the train was routed via Shap; so this would appear to have been a diversion. D5209 is preserved on the Keighley & Worth Valley Railway. (ColourRail.com/A.B. Jeffrey)

81. Stanier Jubilee no. 45690 *Leander* is in fine form with Gordon Hodgson at the regulator as it speeds across bridge no. 306 alongside the Midland Hotel at Lazonby, heading 1Z49 the 08.33 York to Carlisle 'Dalesman' charter on 9th July 2015. The photographer thought that the lack of the usual cars parked at this spot enhanced the scene. (Gordon Edgar)

Baron Wood Tunnels 1 (south) & 2 (north)

Approximately two miles north of Lazonby are the Baron Wood tunnels 1 and 2 that are 207yds (189m) and 251yds (230m) long, respectively.

Baron Wood Sidings

Situated immediately after exiting the northern tunnel, the sidings, complete with a loading dock, were opened for the Ley family of Lazonby Hall to transport products, notably pit props, from the saw mill that made use of the local forest, Baron Wood. The sidings closed in 1951 and the connection to the line severed.

Armathwaite Tunnel

Less than a mile further north of Baron Wood no. 2 is Armathwaite tunnel (325yd (297m) long).

82. The late-running 1Z87 Carlisle to London Euston 'Winter Cumbrian Mountain Express', hauled by Jubilee class no. 45699 *Galatea*, bursts out of Armathwaite tunnel and storms up the 1 in 220 gradient to Baron Wood summit on 8th February 2014. (Gordon Edgar)

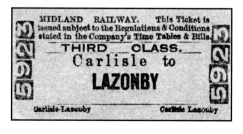

Armathwaite Viaduct

The viaduct has nine arches is 80ft (24m) high and 176yds (161m) long; runs north-south along the River Eden valley and was completed in 1875. It was Grade II listed on 9th March 1984.

83. Class 47 no. 47587 crosses Armathwaite viaduct with a diverted WCML Glasgow - Euston train on the 6th April 1985. To the left of the picture, bridge no. 321 spans the High Hesket to Armathwaite road. The disparity between the height of the parapet to this bridge, which untypically for this line has a pointed arch, and the nine-arch viaduct is thought to be due to the bridge having been constructed in advance of the remainder of the railway. (Noel Machell)

ARMATHWAITE

← *The signal box seen in 1994. (ColourRail.com /David A. Lee)*

XVIII. Opened on 1st May 1876, this station was closed by BR on 5th May 1970 and re-opened on 14th July 1986. With Cotehill, Cumwhinton and Scotby stations closed in the 1950s, Armathwaite was the last stop on the line before Carlisle. The goods facility was taken out of use on 6th April 1964. With closure in 1970, the station buildings on the 'Carlisle' platform were acquired for private use so passenger shelter was constructed at the northern end of the platform. The station signal box was opened on 2nd August 1875; a replacement box opened on 14th July 1895, due to the original box being destroyed by fire, and closed on 5th January 1983. Still owned by Network Rail it was leased to FoSCL in 1992 and it has since been fully restored to its Midland Railway appearance but is not operational. This heritage feature of the line is open for guided tours.

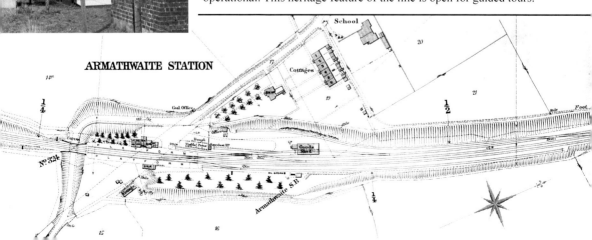

ARMATHWAITE STATION

84. Midland Compound 4-4-0 no. 1000 is approaching the station from the north. (Robert Humm collection)

85. Ex-LMS Ivatt class 4MT 2-6-0 no. 43049 with a three-coach local service. Although undated the shot shows the station buildings still in railway use. (Robert Humm collection)

86. Class 25 no. 25226 passes through the station on a northbound freight train on 17th August 1982. Note the building to the right; it is an extension to the original station building which went into private ownership when the station was closed in the 1970s. (Michael Ellis)

The 'Armathwaite' Landslip

Extremely heavy rain in February 2016 caused a 500,000 tonnes landslip near Armathwaite at Eden Brows that completely blocked the line. As a consequence, services from Armathwaite to Carlisle were suspended from 9th February 2016. Network Rail then embarked on an immense £23m project to reinstate the line, which did not re-open until 30th March 2017; to mark the occasion 12 services were operated by Northern, with trains running between Appleby and Skipton hauled by A1 Pacific no. 60163 *Tornado*.

Dry Beck Viaduct

This seven-arch viaduct, sometimes referred to as Drybeck viaduct, is 80ft (24m) high and 139yd (127m) long. It was Grade II listed on 9th March 1984. Dry by name and dry by nature except in periods of heavy rain and substantial snow melt as was the case when the following photograph was taken. As trains cross the viaduct, they pass between the new non-metropolitan unitary authorities of 'Cumberland' (north) and 'Westmorland and Furness' (south).

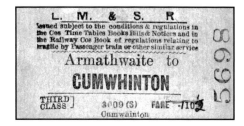

87. The majestic structure actually receives little attention from photographers probably on account of the sun being straight down the line for the usual northbound steam paths, although locomotives are worked hard on the climb. This image on a cloudy-bright day records the Lancaster to Carlisle 'Fellsman' with Stanier '8F' 2-8-0 no. 48151 in charge on 11th July 2012. (Gordon Edgar)

88. The final 'Waverley' charter of the 2012 season, behind Stanier Black 5 4-6-0 no. 45305, is crossing the elegant 80ft (24m) high Dry Beck viaduct near Armathwaite. The was the 1Z73 15.45 Carlisle to York in September 2012. (Gordon Edgar)

Low House Crossing and Signal Box

One of only two crossings on the main line, with the other at Culgaith. Apparently there was another crossing inside the Howe & Co sidings complex. The box was opened on 2nd August 1875 and was replaced by the current box on 14th October 1900 and of course is still in current use.

89. This shot was taken on 3rd June 1989. Across the track is the photographer's car of that vintage, a Volvo, that he claims was far better than all its successors. (Robert Humm collection)

Cotehill Viaduct

Sometimes referred to as the High Stand, after the Gill it passes over, or Knot Hill viaduct, it has four arches, stands at 60ft (18m) and is relatively short at 91yd (83m).

90. On 1st May 1958, Black 5 no. 44754 fitted with Caprotti valve gear on a Carlisle Durran Hill - Stourton fitted freight is seen crossing High Stand viaduct, Cotehill.
(R.H. Leslie/
Peter J. Robinson collection)

➡ *This signpost indicates just how close the wayside stations were to each other.* Flying Scotsman, *then numbered 502, is heading the 14.25 Carlisle to London Euston 'Cumbrian Mountain Express on 6th February 2016 at Duncowfold, near Cotehill.*
(Gordon Edgar)

Robinson's Siding

Immediately before Cotehlll station were the sidings and a tramway to the Knothill gypsum mines and plaster works owned by Robinson & Co. The sidings were disconnected from the national network in 1940.

COTEHILL

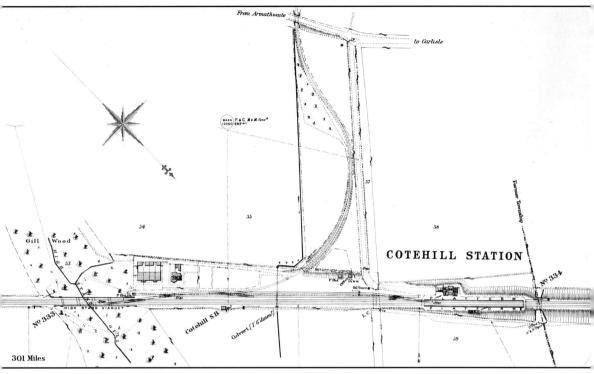

XIX. During the planning stage for construction of the station it was variously referred to as 'Duncowfold', 'High Stand Gill' and 'Knot Mill' - all local landmarks in this part of the Eden Valley. Eventually the name Cotehill was chosen and it opened in 1876 and finally closed on 7th April 1952, as was the goods yard. Unlike other stations on the line, the whole station including the station master's house was demolished. Highstand Gill Signal box was situated closer to Robinson's sidings than the station. It opened on 2nd August 1875, was renamed Knot Hill then Cotehill Station box in 1876; a replacement box opened on 14th August 1904 and was closed in 1952 on or around the same time as the station and was later demolished.

91. A closed but not derelict station photographed from a passing train in April 1974. Cotehill, along with Crosby Garrett, are the only two stations where the station buildings and platforms have been totally demolished. (Alan Young)

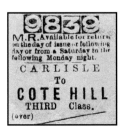

Howe & Co Sidings

About a mile further on various sidings had been established; on the up side a simple siding for what was formerly the Carlisle Brick & Tile Works and, on the down side, sidings and a tramway to the Cocklakes Alabaster mine and mill. Cocklakes mine was the first place to manufacture plasterboard in the UK and the Cocklakes mine even had an underground diesel railway built to assist the moving of raw materials. Activity at the mine increased dramatically during WWII and additional sidings were laid. British Gypsum was the final operator after a series of takeovers. The mine closed on 20th July 1966, although production continued at the mill using imported material, continuing until early 1980 when it became uneconomical. Plant and machinery was removed and the buildings demolished. The siding to the brickworks closed and the track lifted towards the end of 1964. The Howe & Co sidings were disconnected from the national network in 1964 save for the loop that ran in front of the signal box.

Howe & Co Sidings Signal Box

Opened to control access to/from the sidings in 1886, it was reframed on 8th September 1895 and replaced on 17th December 1916. It was again reframed in 1943 to meet the increased wartime activity. The box is currently still in use though it now only controls the main line and is a fringe box to Carlisle Power Signal Box. It is one of a few signal boxes across the network that bears the name of a private company.

92. Jubilee class no. 45690 *Leander* storms the curve past the Howe & Co signal box and siding, heading the Carlisle to York 'Dalesman' on 23rd June 2015. The siding has been used to stable track tamping vehicles. (Gordon Edgar)

CUMWHINTON

XX. Cumwhinton station opened on 1st May 1876 and closed on 5th November 1956. Although designated a 'small' station, according to Midland categories, it did have a station master's house, railway workers' cottages and a goods yard that also closed on 5th November 1956. The station building is now in private ownership and it was Grade II listed on 9th March 1984. The signal box opened on 2nd August 1875, was replaced in 1897 and closed on 1st March 1958; it was demolished some years later.

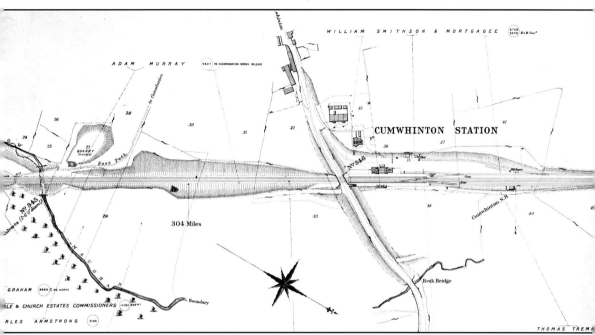

93. The station seen here in September 1920 looking south; the station is looking pristine. (John Alsop collection)

94. Ex-LMS Ivatt class 4MT 2-6-0 no. 43004 is heading north with a local passenger service on 21st July 1965. It did not stop here, of course, the station having closed almost nine years earlier. (ColourRail.com/D. Forsyth)

95. Now returned to its former glory, the listed red sandstone station buildings with a Welsh slate roof show up well, despite the weather. Gresley A3 no. 60103 *Flying Scotsman* is making heavy weather of the 1 in 132 gradient through the former Cumwhinton station, heading the Railway Touring Company's 'The Waverley' charter, 1Z39 16.30 Carlisle to York, on a very wet Sunday 10th September 2023. (Gordon Edgar)

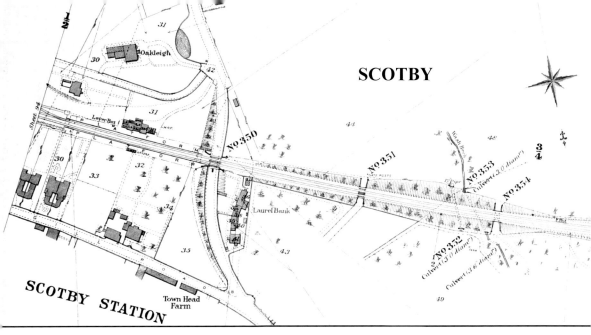

SCOTBY

XXI. There were two stations at the village of Scotby, a few miles outside Carlisle; one served the NER and the other the Settle & Carlisle line as shown in this map and both are now closed. This was the most northerly station on the line that opened on 1st May 1876 and closed on 1st February 1942 along with the goods yard. This was probably due to its close proximity to the NER station and the advent of local bus services. Before closure of Scotby the short distance between it and Cumwhinton beat the Culgaith and New Biggin stretch. The station buildings and station master's house were incorporated into a development running alongside the track. The signal box opened on 2nd August 1875, was replaced in 1897 and closed on 31st October 1909 and was later demolished.

96. Another typically well-kept station on the line looking towards Cumwhinton in this undated photograph. As noted by others, the waiting shelter on the up platform is not of typical Midland design. (Lens of Sutton Assoc.)

Durran Hill South Sidings and Signal Box

XXII. Very soon after leaving Scotby the line reaches Durran Hill South sidings where freight trains were marshalled and the NER from Newcastle appears from the right. The sidings were controlled by the Durran Hill South Sidings signal box, which opened on 16th August 1877, was replaced on 8th November 1891, reframed in 1921 and closed on 12th May 1965, later being demolished.

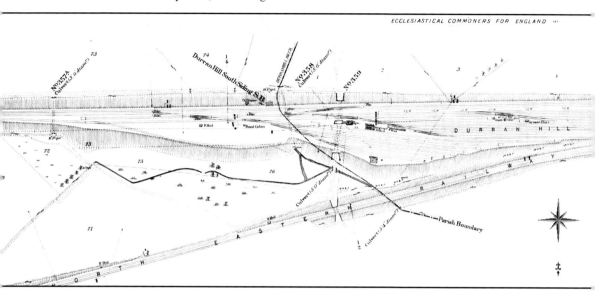

Durran Hill Junction & Signal Box, Petteril Bridge Goods Station & Signal Box and Petteril Junction Signal Box

XXIII. After passing Durran Hill south sidings, in less than half a mile the line reaches Durran Hill Junction; to the left is Durran Hill motive power depot and ahead further extensive freight sidings. Further east is the goods station and ahead Petteril Bridge Junction. The junction signal box opened on 16th August 1877; a replacement box opened on 17th November 1895 and closed on 25th April 1971. The goods signal box opened on 18th November 1891, was reframed in 1920 and temporarily closed on 4th September 1960, no longer functioning as a block post. It closed on 12th November 1961 and was replaced by a ground frame that was demolished in 1965. Petteril Junction box was under the control of NER signalmen. This opened on 20th June 1891 and closed on 3rd June 1973, being later demolished. After closure, the junction came under the control of the Carlisle power box.

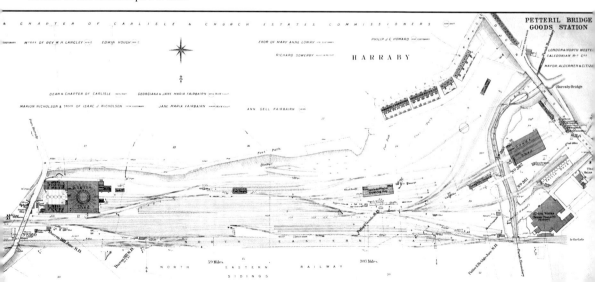

97. In this undated photo the Thames - Clyde Express is seen passing Durran Hill junction box headed by Black 5 no. 44673, which was piloting an unidentified Jubilee. The NER line from Newcastle can just be seen passing behind the signal box. (Robert Humm collection/Eric Treacy)

98. A mixed freight hauled by an unidentified ex-LMS Crab 2-6-0 on a southbound service from Carlisle is seen passing the overgrown remains of Durran Hill sidings, with Keenan Park in the background on 13th June 1964. (Noel Machell)

Durran Hill Motive Power Depot

As seen in map XXIII the depot was located to the north of the line at that point. Opened in 1875 with a brick-built roundhouse, it was about a mile east of Carlisle Citadel station. After the 1923 grouping, the depot was classified as a sub-shed of Carlisle Kingmoor. The shed closed in pre-BR days but re-opened during WWII. Durran Hill motive power depot finally closed on 2nd November 1959.

99. A view of Durran Hill depot taken in August 1900 with a variety of MR locomotives seen on shed. (Robert Humm collection)

100. Compare and contrast: In this photograph, taken in July 1935, there are clearly a number of LMS locomotives on shed. Would the former Midland vehicles alongside the water tank be stored awaiting disposal? (John Alsop collection)

4a. Petteril Bridge to Carlisle Citadel station

This section of the line was not built by the Midland Railway and, at this point, the Settle & Carlisle had running powers over the North Eastern Railway lines into Carlisle Citadel station. The story of the line would not be complete without covering this final part of the journey.

Petteril Bridge Junction

At 72 miles and 46 chains from Settle Junction, Petteril Bridge Junction marks the most northerly point of the Settle to Carlisle line. The S&C and NER had been running in parallel either side of the Durran Hill marshalling yards; the former did not join the NER until this point. This location was once, quite literally, the railway nerve centre for Carlisle with Durranhill, London Road and Upperby sheds, all within 500 yards of this bridge, not to mention numerous yards, warehouses and sidings. Apart from the Grade II listed Midland Railway Goods shed, virtually lost in the birch trees behind where the photographer was standing, this delightful bridge is really now the only reminder here of those times past.

101. The rain was falling in stair rods, not unusual for Cumbria, but the main source of light to the east produced a glint not normally associated with a mid-afternoon shot facing in that direction. With his firing work completed for a brief interlude, the fireman of Stanier Black 5 no.44932 attentively watches the road ahead as 1Z73 the 15.45 Carlisle to York 'The Waverley' charter takes the Midland route off to the right at Petteril Bridge Junction, heading for the 'Roof of England' and York and potentially better weather than experienced in Carlisle during the afternoon of 26th August 2012. The line to Hexham and Newcastle runs directly ahead of the train. (Gordon Edgar)

102. 'Green, at last...' Northbound coal empties off the Settle & Carlisle line finally get the all clear after a lengthy hold up at Petteril Bridge Junction on 26th February 2007. At the head of the train is Freightliner class 66 no. 66549. The land beyond the trees on the left was once occupied by the Midland Railway's Durranhill Yard and Goods Station now part of Durran Hill Industrial Estate. (John Furnevel)

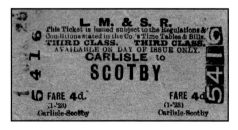

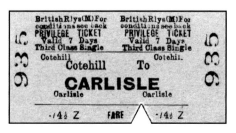

Petteril Bridge Accident

On the 19th October 2022 five tank wagons loaded with cement powder on the Clitheroe - Mossend service derailed near Petteril Bridge Junction. A number of wagons were damaged, while there was also considerable damage to the track and the River Petteril bridge. Two of the derailed wagons fell off the side of the bridge and one went into the river. This resulted in closure of both routes from Carlisle to Newcastle and Settle for seven weeks. There were no injuries.

↗ 103. A close up of the pumping operation at Petteril Bridge Junction on 28th October 2022. This was to empty the cement tankers before they were removed or cut up on site. The cement powder is being pumped via pipes over the tracks to road tankers out of view on the left. This shot is looking east with the line to Newcastle straight ahead. In this foreshortened view, the S&C branches off to the right immediately behind the stricken tankers and can be seen passing under the road bridge in the top right of the picture. (Duncan Ross)

➔ *These are the two wagons that fell off the bridge as a result of the derailment. (Duncan Ross)*

London Road Tunnel

Just before the tunnel, the NER line terminated at London Road station; it closed on 1st January 1863 and services continued on to Citadel station. The building is now a warehouse and trains off the Settle-Carlisle and Tyne Valley Lines still pass immediately to the south of the site of the former station. Just beyond, the line passes under London Road through a short tunnel.

104. On 23rd October 2013, Jubilee class no. 45699 *Galatea* is seen opening up just clear of London Road tunnel. It is heading the return 'Cumbrian Mountain Express' to London Euston via the Settle-Carlisle line, with electric traction taking over at Farington Junction, south of Preston, and this time working without the assistance of a 'fire-risk' diesel. Note there is no excursion headboard on the locomotive. (Gordon Edgar)

Carlisle South Junction

This is the junction where the Settle-Carlisle and Tyne Valley Lines merge with the West Coast Mainline just south of Carlisle Citadel station.

105. Deeley Superheated Class 4 no. 998 is taking the south curve with a London St Pancras and Bristol Temple Meads express in September 1912. The LNWR route will be under the gantry seen behind the second and third coaches. (John Alsop collection)

↓ 106. This shot puts the previous image into perspective. A class 47 with a down WCML express is about to run into Carlisle station some time in September 1971, having just passed over a freight heading for London Road junction on the Carlisle goods lines. An unidentified class 40 with a parcels train from Newcastle is held at the signals on the climb up to the station, awaiting the passing of the express. The train in the previous picture would have been descending on the up line adjacent to where the parcels train is standing. The substantial bridge supports seen across the shot once carried the lines into Crown Street goods depot closed in 1966. (John Furnevel)

107. A very different picture today. The class 66 no. 66423, in Direct Rail Services livery, is on the single bi-directional track between Carlisle South Junction and London Road Junction, where double track recommences. This now single line feeds both the Settle & Carlisle and Tyne Valley lines. The track visible alongside the 66 is now a long siding from Carlisle South Junction, known as the 'NE Shunt Neck'. This is electrified and Transpennine EMUs have been seen stabled there. The siding was once the up line along this section. The 66 is hauling 6K05 the 12.46 Carlisle Yard to Crewe Basford Hall Yard engineers service, which at the time ran Monday-Friday via the Settle & Carlisle, Hellifield, Blackburn, Lostock Hall and Farington Junction. (Martyn Hilbert)

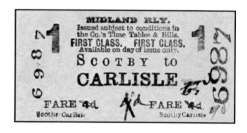

Other views of this area can be seen in *Hexham to Carlisle,* *Carlisle to Hawick* **and** *Carlisle to Beattock.*

CARLISLE CITADEL

Carlisle Citadel station is on the West Coast Main Line 102 miles (164 km) southeast of Glasgow Central and 299 miles (481 km) northwest of London Euston. It is the northern terminus of the Settle and Carlisle Line, a continuation of the Midland Main Line from Leeds, Sheffield and London St Pancras. Designed by architect, William Tite, the station opened on 1st September 1847 to accommodate the Lancaster & Carlisle and Caledonian Railways, the original owners of the station. Between 1875 and 1876, the station was expanded to accommodate the lines of other companies of which the Midland Railway was the seventh railway company to use it. Over the centuries, the station has been the subject of expansion, perpetual repair and maintenance, restoration and continued modernisation, including electrification that enabled full through electric services from London to Glasgow that started on 6th May 1974. The station was Grade II listed in November 1972 and, in April 1994, the freestanding retaining wall was also listed separately as Grade II.

108. The Grade II listed station façade as seen on 15th November 2014. (ColourRail.com/Paul Chancellor)

XXIV. The route into Carlisle Citadel station is shown in red on this 25ins to 1 mile map of 1926. The line passes through the London Road tunnel (picture no. 105) and then under the line to the former Crown Street goods depot (no. 107) before taking the south curve (no. 108) before reaching the throat of Citadel station.

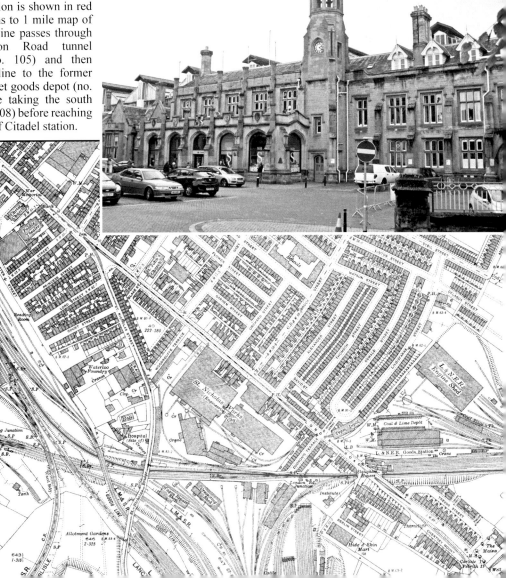

109. On 10th September 1960, 'The Waverley' headed Black 5 no. 45481 piloting Royal Scot class no. 46117 *Welsh Guardsman* ready to depart at 10.05. To the left is another Black 5 no. 45452 and, almost out of view, is an English Electric class 40. Note the retaining wall that was Grade II listed in 1994. (Robert Humm collection)

110. BR class 46 'Peak' 1Co-co1 no. D181 (TOPS 46044) arrives with the down 'Thames - Clyde Express' on 28th August 1971. The bay-windowed two-storey edifice to the right of the train is Carlisle signal box 4a. (Tom Heavyside)

Ex-LMS Silver Jubilee class no. 45593 Kolhapur, nameplates removed, stands at the north end of platform 3 awaiting to depart with a Leeds - Glasgow summer season Saturdays-only train on 7th August 1965. The locomotive was one of the last of its class in service soldiering on until mid October 1967. These locos worked out of Leeds Holbeck depot on the Settle & Carlisle line for approximately 30 years. (Noel Machell)

111. A midsummer steam charter train arrival under the overall roof is extremely well-lit on a sunny day. Such a spectacle adds further charm to an already delightful period survivor. Members of the public are clearly amazed at the arrival of K4 no. 61994 *The Great Marquess* as it wheezes into platform 3 after what was understood to be a troublesome run for the footplate crew from Lancaster via the S&C hauling 'The Fellsman' charter on 19th June 2013. (Gordon Edgar)

5. Hawes Junction to Hawes
6 Miles (9.7km)

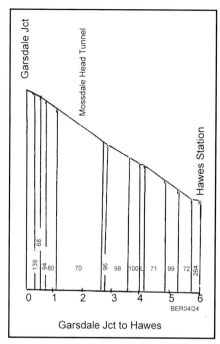

Garsdale Jct to Hawes

The contract for this section in the sum of £84,000 was awarded to Messrs Benton and Woodiwiss in mid-1871 and employed up to 350 men.

The line opened on 1st October 1878; it closed to passengers on 16th March 1959 and goods in April 1964. Most of the passenger services were operated by the NER later the LNER.

The line to Hawes is a microcosm of the main Settle & Carlisle line inasmuch that in six miles it boasts a tunnel, two viaducts and a station.

112. Ex-LMS Fairburn class 4MT 2-6-4T no. 42491 stands in the Hawes branch platform on 18th May 1959 with the 4.40pm Garsdale - Hellifield stopping train. This was the rump of the 'Bonniface' services that previously ran to/from Hawes. (Cumbrian Railways Association Mayor collection ref MAY006)

Mossdale Head Tunnel

A single-track bore of 245yd (224m), both portals have wing walls and buttresses either side of the entrance. Internally, the tunnel has been distorted due to surrounding ground movement. The long-term aspirations of the Wensleydale Railway involve the reconnection of its railhead at Redmire with the Settle & Carlisle at Garsdale; such a scheme is likely to be prohibitively costly given problems at Redmire, let alone the remedial work required on the tunnel. At one stage, the abandoned tunnel had been used for storing farming equipment.

Mossdale Viaduct

Mossdale Viaduct, also known as Mossdale Gill Viaduct, is 78yd (72m) long, 40ft (12.2m) high and has four arches. Construction work commenced in June 1876 and the structure was completed in February 1878.

113. A view taken on 5th August 1969. Note that different stone has been used on the parapet. Through the arch is one of the two Mossdale Beck waterfalls. (J. Marshall/Kidderminster Railway Museum)

Appersett Viaduct

Appersett Viaduct is 108yd (99m) long, 80ft (24.4m) high and has five arches. Construction work commenced on 28th November 1873, together with the adjacent embankments, and was completed in June 1878. It crossed over Widdale Beck; the viaduct is Grade II listed.

114. A partial view of the viaduct taken on 15th April 1999 showing the majority of the arches. (G. Biddle/Kidderminster Railway Museum)

HAWES

115. A busy station but sadly undated. Note the MR wagons in the yard to the rear of the station building. (Robert Humm collection)

XXV. This 1912 25ins to 1 mile OS map shows the full extent of Hawes station and its goods yard. Built by the MR in fairly typical style, and opened in October 1878, the station was the terminus of the 6 mile (9.7km) branch from Garsdale, or Hawes Junction, as then was. The NER line from Northallerton through Bedale, and later Leyburn, was extended to Hawes in 1878 to form an end-on junction with the MR. While the station was MR owned the NER operated almost all passenger services through to Garsdale, hence the NER locomotives recorded earlier at that station. There was one notable exception and that was the daily return service between Hawes and Hellifield that had the curious nickname 'Bonnyface', supposedly dreamt up by railway workmen.

The LNER section of the line lost its passenger services in April 1954 but the LMS ran a daily shuttle between Hawes and Garsdale until cessation of all passenger services on the branch, on 16th March 1959. Goods traffic continued for a few years until complete closure of the line on 27th April 1964, after which the track was lifted and buildings left to the mercy of the elements. The signal box, seen to the east of the station, opened on 22nd June 1878. It was replaced on 12th August 1900, renamed Hawes Station SB on 14th April 1907, closed in 1959 and was later demolished. The West signal box opened on 22nd June 1878, was replaced on 9th September 1900 and closed in April 1907. After some years, the Yorkshire Dales National Park Authority purchased the site and converted it in the 1990s. The station buildings now house the Dales Countryside Museum, sited in the old railway station. In 2015, a section of the building was rented to a business running a bicycle shop and café.

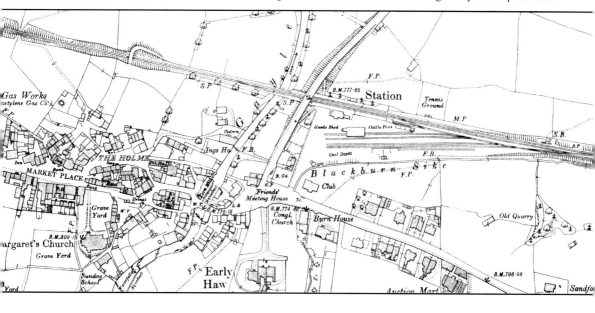

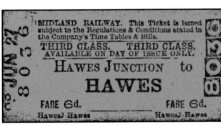

116. In this undated photo an MR Kirtley outside frame 0-6-0 no. 2716 is seen passing through the station with a mixed freight. (Robert Humm collection)

117. An extremely busy station and goods yard as seen on 5th September 1953. (Lens of Sutton Association)

118. A somewhat crowded station with passengers showing a lot of interest; perhaps the locomotive is being re-coupled after running round its train. The locomotive was an ex-LMS Stanier class 4MT 2-6-4T no. 42492. This shot was taken on 14th March 1959 only two days before the line was closed to passengers and, being a Saturday, it was bound to be an attraction. (ColourRail.com)

119. An almost deserted, but certainly rundown, station and rusted tracks seen some time after closure of the line in 1964. (ColourRail.com/R. Oakley)

120. Part of the museum scheme involved not only renovating the station buildings but also relaying some track in the vicinity. An industrial tank engine, posing as an LNER locomotive, is a static exhibit together with three BR Mark 1 coaches, as seen in this shot taken on 27th April 2019. The locomotive was not built by the LNER but by Robert Stephenson & Hawthorn in 1955; works no. 7845 was once of CEGB Hams Hall power station in Warwickshire. (Gordon Edgar)

First verse and chorus of The Settle and Carlisle *song, by Dave Goulder.*

**The Settle Carlisle Railway was built into the land
More viaducts and tunnels than the lines upon your hand
She cuts across the Pennines over water, rock and air
Seventy miles of monument to the men who put her there**

**Well, I'd like to sit awhile, by the Settle and Carlisle
And delve among the memories at evening…**